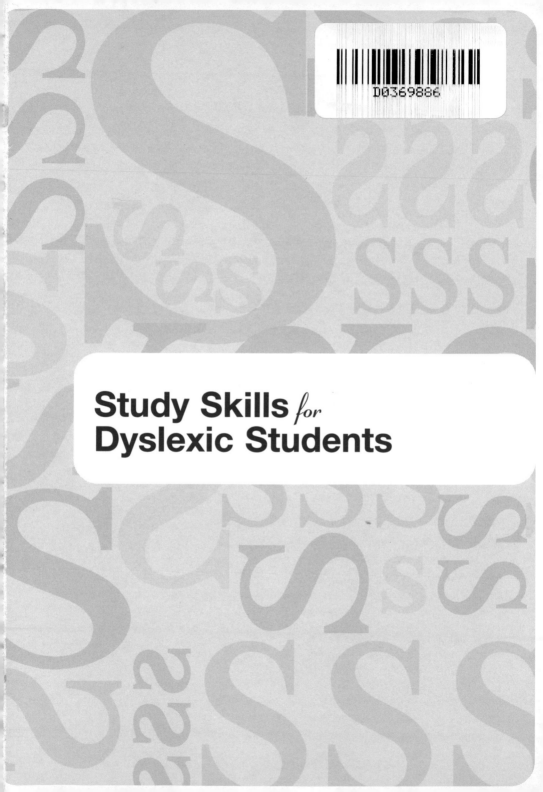

Study Skills *for* Dyslexic Students

Study Skills *for* Dyslexic Students

Edited by **Sandra Hargreaves**

Los Angeles • London • New Delhi • Singapore • Washington DC

KH

First published 2007

Reprinted 2008

SAGE Publications Ltd
1 Oliver's Yard
55 City Road
London EC1Y 1SP

SAGE Publications Inc.
2455 Teller Road
Thousand Oaks, California 91320

SAGE Publications India Pvt Ltd
B 1/I 1 Mohan Cooperative Industrial Area
Mathura Road, New Delhi 110 044
India

SAGE Publications Asia-Pacific Pte Ltd
33 Pekin Street #02-01
Far East Square
Singapore 048763

British Library Cataloguing in Publication data

A catalogue record for this book is available from the
British Library

ISBN 978-1-4129-3608-8
ISBN 978-1-4129-3609-5 (pbk)

Library of Congress Control Number: 2007924721

Typeset by C&M Digitals (P) Ltd, Chennai, India
Printed in Great Britain by The Cromwell Press, Trowbridge, Wiltshire
Printed on paper from sustainable resources

8/28/09

Contents

About the CD-ROM

A CD-ROM accompanies the book which contains:

- The whole text of the book in Microsoft Word. This has been done to make the book as accessible as possible for dyslexic students and those with other Specific Learning Difficulties. This allows you to:
    - have the text of the book read out to you using a text reader such as ClaroRead Plus 2007, TextHELP Read & Write or Kurzweil.
    - change the colour of the background, font style and size (see Chapter 11, 'How ICT Can Help You')
- Student planners, essay templates and like materials supplied as Word, Excel files, etc. so that you can copy and edit them.
- A number of internet shortcuts for each chapter which you can investigate if you want further information, templates and additional help.

Throughout the book, you will see this CD icon used (⊙). This indicates that there is electronic material available on the accompanying CD-ROM.

CD-ROM contents

How to Use This Book

ABC Study Guide Index	Internet Shortcut
Study Guides and Strategies	Internet Shortcut

Chapter 1 – Managing Your Workload

Blank Weekly Planner	Excel Template
Colour Coded Assignment List – An Example	Word Document
To Do List	Word Document
Weekly Planner Template	Excel Template
Weekly Planner First Example	Example of use
Weekly Planner Second Example	Example of use
Weekly Planner Template (Excel) Instructions	Directions to use Excel Template
Weekly Planner Template (Word).doc	Word Template
Weekly Planner Semester 1 First Example	Word Document
Weekly Planner Semester 1 Second Example	Word Document
Weekly Planner Template (Word) Instructions	Directions to use Word Template
Year Planner	Excel Template
Time Management	Internet Shortcut
Virginia Tech Study Skills Self-help Information	Internet Shortcut

Chapter 2 – Understanding Your Preferred Learning Style

KnowitAll	Internet Shortcut
VARK – A Guide to Learning Styles	Internet Shortcut

Chapter 3 – Note Taking and Note Making

Four Quarter System Template	Word Document
Four Quarter System Example	Word Document

Owl at Purdue	Internet Shortcut
Writing/Reflections – Shenandoah University	Internet Shortcut

Chapter 7 – Improving your Grammar, Spelling and Punctuation

Conjunctive Adverbs	Word Document
Eight Parts of Speech	Internet Shortcut
More Pronouns	Word Document
Punctuation Exercises	Word Document
Look-Say-Cover-Write-Check Template	Word Document
BBC Skillswise	Internet Shortcut
Blue Book of Grammar and Punctuation	Internet Shortcut
English Grammar Card by Joseph Donovan	Internet Shortcut
Fifty Writing Tips for Journalists	Internet Shortcut
Grammar Girl's Quick and Dirty Tips for Better Writing	Internet Shortcut
Grammarama	Internet Shortcut
Most Difficult Words to Spell	Internet Shortcut
Prefixes, Suffixes & Syllables	Internet Shortcut
Punctuation Made Simple	Internet Shortcut
Word Families – Prefixes	Internet Shortcut
Word Families – Suffixes	Internet Shortcut

Chapter 8 – Improving Mathematics Skills and Using Statistics

Adding Fractions	Word Document
Answers to 3M Questions	Word Document
BBC Skillswise	Internet Shortcut

Chapter 9 – Examination Techniques

Chapter 11 – How ICT Can Help You

Microsoft Office Online	Internet Shortcut
Microsoft Training Manuals – EBIT Solutions	Internet Shortcut
Nuance Hardware Compatibility List	Internet Shortcut
Open Office Forum	Internet Shortcut
Sams Teach Yourself Microsoft Windows XP in 24 Hours	Internet Shortcut
Serif Software – Drawplus 4	Internet Shortcut
SourceForge.net	Internet Shortcut
The 46 Best-ever Freeware Utilities	Internet Shortcut
Voice Recognition Forum	Internet Shortcut
Windows XP Accessibility Resources	Internet Shortcut

Editor and Contributors

About the editor

Sandra Hargreaves is the Course Leader for the Postgraduate Certificate in Teaching Adult Dyslexic Learners in Higher Education and the Postgraduate Diploma in Assessment for Specific Learning Difficulties (Dyslexia) at London Metropolitan University. She also operates a consultancy, 'Mind Aligned', which covers a range of different activities including diagnosing dyslexia and supporting dyslexic adults both in higher education and in the workplace. Prior to that she was involved in dyslexia support at Thames Valley University, Uxbridge College and the Inner London Probation Service. Sandra previously worked for many years in Australia at Macquarie University in Sydney in the Teacher Education Programme where she was the Course Leader of the Secondary English Team.

About the contributors

All contributors completed the Postgraduate Certificate: Teaching Adult Dyslexic Learners in Higher Education at London Metropolitan University and are all working as dyslexia tutors in London universities.

Peri Batliwala is a dyslexia support tutor at Middlesex University and has also worked at London School of Hygiene and Tropical Medicine and Queen Mary London. She started her professional life working for International Development Charities as an administrator and sub-editor for many years. After having a family she undertook higher degrees and retrained as a secondary English teacher, a basic skills tutor and most recently, a dyslexia support tutor.

Helen Birkmyre works as a freelance dyslexia tutor at Goldsmiths College London and The Dyslexia Teaching Centre in Kensington. She read history at Goldsmiths and completed an MA in Cultural History. She completed her Postgraduate Certificate in Dyslexia Tutoring at London Metropolitan.

John Brennan is a dyslexia support tutor at University of the South Bank and Kingston University. After education at Downside and Brasenose College, Oxford John worked in IT until 1999 in London with significant periods in Belgium and Holland. Two of the more interesting projects John worked on were the traffic management systems for the Channel Tunnel terminals (www.logicacmg.com/ pdf/industry/ChannelTunnel.pdf) and Wester Schelde estuary (www.scheldenet.nl/? url=/nl/economie/ scheldevaart/veiligheid/wsradarketen/).

Judith Cattermole works part time as a dyslexia support tutor for students at Middlesex and City Universities in London. She has a particular interest in helping dyslexic students who are experiencing problems with their numeracy skills. In addition Judith works as a senior manager in Learning Resources at Middlesex University and is a qualified librarian with over 30 years of experience.

Paula Dawson works both as an administrator in dyslexia support at Kingston University and as a dyslexia support tutor at University of the Southbank. She is from New Zealand and has been living in London for five years. She also has qualifications in English and a Trinity Certificate in Teaching English to Speakers of Other Languages (TESOL). She is currently working towards an MA specialising in Specific Learning Difficulties at London Metropolitan University.

Kay McEachran works part time as a dyslexic support tutor at Middlesex University, Queen Mary London and University of the South Bank as well as part time as a health and safety administrator at London Metropolitan University. Kay was born in Scotland but educated in East London taking her first degree in History at Goldsmiths College London and a Masters in Politics and Government from London Guildhall University.

Acknowledgements

Every effort has been made to seek permission where material has been known to come from specific sources. The following permissions are gratefully acknowledged:

Diagram of Cognitive Styles and Learning Strategies (p. 12) reproduced by kind permission from *Cognitive Styles and Learning Strategies* by Richard Riding and Stephen Rayner, David Fulton Publishers, 1998, p. 98.

References to Mind Maps™ (pp. 14ff.) reproduced by kind permission from *The Mind Map Book* (rev. edition) by Tony Buzan with Barry Buzan, BBC Active, 2006.

Visual Memory Pegs (p. 16) reproduced by kind permission from *Make the Most of Your Mind* (rev. edition) by Tony Buzan, Pan Books, 1988.

Auditory Memory Pegs (p. 17) reproduced by kind permission from *Use Your Head* (4th edition) by Tony Buzan, BBC, 1985.

The Cornell Note-making System (p. 30) reproduced by kind permission from *How to Study in College* (7th edition) by Walter Pauk, Houghton Mifflin, 2001, p. 201

Q Notes Template (p. 31) reproduced by kind permission from *Tools for Thought* by Jim Burke, Heinemann, 2002.

The Point Evidence Comment method of paragraph writing (chapter 6) reproduced by kind permission from *The Good History Student's Handbook,* edited by Gilbert Pleuger, Sempringham, 2000.

Abstract Writing (p. 76) reproduced by kind permission from the Online Writing Lab of Purdue University.

There are many people whom I would like to thank who have been indispensable to the development and production of this book. First my grateful thanks are due to all the contributors, who gave their time to develop chapters on topics in which they had expertise. My special thanks go to John Brennan who was responsible for the systematic lay-out of the chapters at the draft stages and his patient advice regarding all aspects of ICT. Secondly I am greatly indebted to all the students who have used the strategies in this book and who have been willing to write and speak about their experiences in the case studies. I would also like to thank both Jude Bowen and Sophie Cox for their honest but supportive comments and advice during the editorial process. Finally I would like to thank all my family and friends who have unstintingly supported my efforts on this book and for their unswerving belief that I would complete it.

This book is dedicated to dyslexic students and those with other Specific Learning Difficulties who have struggled with the demands of student life. I hope that the strategies we have suggested will bring success.

Sandra Hargreaves

How to use this book

This book is for students with dyslexia and has been designed to be used independently. It provides strategies to help dyslexic students and those with other Specific Learning Difficulties such as dyspraxia but would also be helpful for a wide range of students, for what is specifically useful for dyslexic students is useful for everyone. If you would like more information about learning difficulties, you should approach the Disability and Dyslexia Service at your college. As well as giving help and material resources, these services will assist you to apply for the Disabled Students' Allowance (DSA) if you are eligible for it.

www.direct.gov.uk/en/DisabledPeople/EducationAndTraining/HigherEducation/DG_10034898

It is always a good idea to be pro-active about your learning difficulties and to inform your lecturers and tutors so that they can adjust their teaching practices by providing notes (preferably in digital format) and prioritised reading lists in advance and allowing the use of recorders. Remember that you are not asking for favours, but for your rights under the Disability Act. Your lecturers and tutors have an obligation to make 'reasonable adjustments' to accommodate your individual needs.

http://www.nottingham.ac.uk/academicsupport

A CD-ROM accompanies the book which contains:

- The whole text of the book in Microsoft Word. This has been done to make the book as accessible as possible for dyslexic students and those with other Specific Learning Difficulties. This allows you to:

    - have the text of the book read out to you using a text reader such as ClaroRead Plus 2007, TextHELP Read & Write or Kurzweil.
    - change the colour of the background, font style and size (see Chapter 11, 'How ICT Can Help You')

- Student planners, essay templates and like materials supplied as Word, Excel files, etc. so that you can copy and edit them.
- A number of internet shortcuts for each chapter which you can investigate if you want further information, templates and additional help.

The colour background of the book itself has been designed for dyslexic students, who often find that it is hard to read black text on a white background. You can change the background colour of the text in this book, if it doesn't suit you, by using a coloured overlay. Try different colours to see which suits you by trialling different coloured plastic folders.

The text has been **emboldened** in sections, which appears as a contrasting colour on the CD. The purpose is twofold, to:

- enable you to **scan** (see Chapter 4, 'Reading Strategies and Speed Reading') the book for the **main ideas**,
- encourage you to use **highlighting** as a note-making **technique** (see Chapter 3, 'Note Taking and Note Making').

Colour has been used throughout the text and in a number of figures. The colour version of the text is available on the accompanying CD-ROM.

This book is a collection of **strategies** and **techniques** (such as **highlighting**) which have been collected over many years and from many sources. I hope that they will help you and that having compiled them into a study guide you will have the strategies at your disposal to cope with the academic demands of your course. The book is an edited collection of chapters containing strategies from a range of tutors. All the strategies have been trialled and found to be successful. All the contributors have completed the Postgraduate Certificate: Teaching Adult Dyslexic Learners in Higher Education at London Metropolitan University.

The book has been designed to help students with the demands of college or university life. As such, it allows readers to select according to their immediate needs. So you can go to Chapter 5, 'Answering Essay Questions' if you need help with a forthcoming essay, or to Chapter 6, 'Structuring Different Writing Genres' for a report. You may find, however, that by systematically reading the whole book your organisation and study strategies will generally improve, and you will not feel under so much pressure as you approach deadlines.

This material has been used over many years, and it is not always possible to know where it originated and who should be acknowledged for the original idea. In some cases I have observed the strategies being used with dyslexic students by excellent tutors working in the field and I would like to acknowledge all the useful work that goes on in dyslexia tutorials all over the country.

The aim of the book is as Alan Bennett says so effectively through the voice of the English teacher at the end of *The History Boys*: 'Pass it on … Pass it on'. That surely is the aim of all good education so that those who have learnt the skills can share them with those who have not as yet encountered them.

A final point to remember – Don't let yourself become overwhelmed by the demands of your education. Don't give up but try another strategy, another way to learn something new. I am dyslexic. I only found out I was dyslexic when I moved to the UK and started to work in this field. The more I worked with dyslexic adults, the more I realised that I had experienced the same problems since childhood, many of which I have managed to overcome using some of the strategies now incorporated in this book.

Sandra Hargreaves AMBDA FRSA
BA Dip Ed MA M Ed ADS Cert

Foreword

The concept of the 'dyslexia-friendly school' was devised several years ago by the British Dyslexia Association, and there have been significant improvements in awareness of dyslexia in compulsory education. The numbers of dyslexic university students reported increased tenfold between 1994 and 2004 and there has undoubtedly been a similar increase in Further Education, but neither the truly dyslexia-friendly college nor its Higher Education equivalent has yet emerged.

In spite of this, universities and colleges are enrolling determined and hard-working dyslexic students. They deserve a set of truly inclusive learning and teaching practices which make the curriculum accessible to all.

The existence of the type of brain which is currently called dyslexic is a challenge to the education system as a whole. Meanwhile, students need this book. Written by a group of experienced, wise and empathetic tutors, it covers the key areas of student life in an approachable and user-friendly manner. It aims to enable students to be independent. The book models good practice in several ways, notably by supplying a CD. It will be helpful and informative for all students, regardless of identification as dyslexic.

David Pollak PhD PGCE AMBDA FHEA
Principal Lecturer in Learning Support
National Teaching Fellow
De Montfort University

1 Managing Your Workload

Sandra Hargreaves

This chapter:

- outlines the overall structure of student life including the main things you have to consider;
- suggests ways of planning your workload so that you can complete assignments on time, and still enjoy some leisure and exercise;
- provides examples and templates of weekly and semester timetables (CD-ROM);
- provides templates of helpful forms such as 'To do' lists (CD-ROM).

Student lifestyle

If you have never been to college or university before, you will find it a very great change from the more organised environment of secondary school. Apart from your timetabled lectures, tutorials, seminars and examinations, **how you organise yourself will be up to you**. If you don't organise yourself early in your student life, you can find that you get very behind in all your commitments and this can lead to stress and low morale as well as the possibility of failing modules, resubmissions and resits. Remember, an **organised student is a successful student**.

You may need to extend or develop **better systems of organisation** to support you through your course and it would be useful to talk about these with a tutor. There are more suggestions offered later in this chapter. When you have to learn new material or processes, you will find learning and committing to memory is made easier if you use **multi-sensory methods**. This means that as many of the senses as possible need to be employed in the learning. Remember that colour, image, sound, the use of the voice, mnemonics (auditory devices, such as rhymes or catchy phrases which act as important aids to recall information), story lines, visual displays, 'timelines', etc. can all play a useful part in supporting memory (see Chapter 2, 'Understanding Your Preferred Learning Style').

Main features of student life

- Weekly lectures.
- Weekly tutorials, seminars, practical sessions or workshops.
- Assignments which include coursework essays, reports, and other forms of written work depending on your course.
- Examinations in some subjects and courses.

The amount of time that these scheduled activities take depends on the course that you are doing. If you are doing a **science** course of some kind, your scheduled activities will take up more of your weekly timetable, as you will be involved in a lot of practical work in laboratories. If you are doing an **arts** or **humanities** course, there will be far fewer scheduled activities as you will be required to do a lot of reading and writing in various forms in your own time. If you organise yourself well to cover this work, and to plan to your deadlines, you will not fall behind.

Meeting your deadlines

It is essential to plan ahead for all your deadlines and it is suggested that you try to have a **lead up time of about six weeks** for a major assignment such as a 5,000-word essay. You can write the preparation stages into your semester or term timetable and ensure that you are working on the assignment in the time slots that you have allocated for that subject in your weekly timetable. This can be made easier by colour coding your modules (see CD-ROM) so that you can see the time slots you have allocated across both timetables at a glance. With a 5,000-word essay you should begin to analyse the question about 6 weeks before and allocate your workload into 'chunks' over the next 6 weeks. If your dyslexia support tutor is available, you can go through the various stages of preparation with assistance. A typical plan for such an essay would be:

- 'unpacking the question';
- brainstorming/concept mapping;
- writing a theme to give you direction;
- organising the concept map into sequential paragraphs; and finally
- writing the essay in workable 'chunks'.

All of this will be covered in Chapter 5 but it is imperative to plan early and to allow time to write assignments with plenty of time to cover the required reading and to complete sections of work to discuss with your dyslexia tutor or to review independently. **It is essential to plan in advance and not leave things to the last minute**. If you do, you will be able to review your work properly and you will avoid becoming stressed and overtired.

Ways of planning your workload

There are several strategies that you can use to help you plan your workload which are illustrated in this chapter. Useful tools include:

- a colour coded list of assignments;
- weekly timetables;
- semester or term planners (depending on how your college or unversity operates);
- a 'To do' list.

The CD-ROM that accompanies this book contains templates and guidance on how to adapt them to your own needs. The case study and examples on the following pages are provided by Jane, a Human Nutrition and Dietetics student, who adopted a range of planning strategies. Jane created all the examples herself and found that this approach to organisation completely changed her life at university.

CASE STUDY

Having stumbled my way through a foundation/access course I was first diagnosed with dyslexia in 2003 just before being accepted onto a BSc (Hons) programme for Human Nutrition and Dietetics.

After several consultations with a dyslexic tutor, I began to understand just how dyslexia was affecting me psychologically as well as affecting my work. I was shown various strategies to help organise my workload. From these early tutorials I started to play around with my computer and eventually developed my own long-term planner so that I could visualise at a glance what objectives and deadlines I had to meet over the forthcoming 12 weeks (semester). I also created a weekly timetable, which remained fixed for the first half of the semester but as deadlines were met and obligations fulfilled, it was adapted so as to devote more time to the most immediate deadlines looming. I compiled a list of all coursework deadlines, which I also handed out to my peers. This helped us to see the running order of deadlines and thus prioritise timetables, reading lists and group meetings for further discussion. I particularly enjoyed drawing a thick black line through each piece of work listed as I worked my way down the list. I kept all three organisational pieces on my wall by my PC table. This meant that they were all next to my head throughout the semester and were a constant reminder/motivator. Having organised myself in such a way that I understand and can relate to with ease, I have found that I no longer repeat the 3 a.m. twilight hours experience of rushing work to meet the deadline. Consequently, I have time to check over my work and adapt it, as I feel necessary. I no longer feel as though I'm simply stumbling through my workload without realising the knowledge gained.

My confidence has been restored and this is reflected in my work. I am currently on course to achieve an upper 2:1 and am feeling confident enough to apply myself to try and aim for a first class degree.

A colour coded list of assignments

The first of Jane's strategies is a colour coded list of assignments including presentations, essays and reports.

(GO to Colour Coded Assignment List – an Example on CD-ROM)

The colour coding relates to her four modules and she keeps to this colour coding throughout all her planning strategies. She uses four basic striking colours to distinguish the modules: pink, blue, yellow and green. The list has been compiled in Microsoft Word.

Points of good practice
(See Figure 1.1) Notice that Jane has:

- used a large font which she likes, in this case Comic Sans;
- been consistent in her use of colour;
- scored out completed work; this gives her a sense of achievement and draws attention to the next item on the list.

Weekly timetables and semester or term planners

(GO to Weekly Planners on CD-ROM)

You will see that the same colours appear in Jane's weekly timetables (Figures 1.2 and 1.3) and also in her semester or term planner (Figure 1.4). Microsoft Excel was used to produce the timetable and planners. Microsoft Outlook is also a useful planning program and can be linked in with a personal digital assistant (PDA) if you have one. (All these programs and how they can help you are outlined in Chapter 11.) Initially you can use the basic formats provided on the CD-ROM as long as you have Microsoft Office loaded onto your machine.

November '05

WK 6

~~Thursday 10th   ND 205:   Poster / Diet craze (15 mins...timed)~~

~~(Joanne, Rebecca, Lindsey)~~

WK 8

Friday 25th   ND 211:   Practical Report

DECEMBER '05

WK 10

Friday 9th   ND 214:   Case Study (3000-5000 words)

Friday 9th   ND 214:   Poster Presentation (Based on Case Study)

WK 11

Tuesday 13th   ND211:   Group Presentation (10 mins total)

(Rebecca, Caroline, Lindsey, Joanne)

Friday 16th   FC 220:   Group Report (1500 words) & Presentation

(Caroline, Rebecca, Lindsey, Joanne, Neil, Suman)

Friday 16th   ND 205:   Critical Review. (1500 words)

JANUARY '06

WK 12

Friday 13th   FC 220:   Essay (2000 words)

Figure 1.1   Colour Coded Assignment List – An Example

Figure 1.2 Weekly Planner – Semester 1

Time	Monday	Tuesday	Wednesday	Thursday	Friday	Saturday	Sunday
9	ND 214 Lecture	ND 211 Lecture	1.5 hrs	ND 205 Lecture	2 hrs		2 hrs
10			Break		Break		Break
11			2 hrs		1.5 hrs		1.5 hrs
12	Lunch	Lunch	Lunch	Lunch	Lunch		Lunch
1pm	Dyslexia / Journey home			Journey home		Day Off Work	
2	2 hrs	Library / FC 220 Lecture	1.5 hrs		1.5 hrs		1.5 hrs
3			Break	2 hrs	Break		Break
4		Journey home	2 hrs	Break			
5	Dinner	Dinner		1.5 hrs	2 hrs		2 hrs
6	1.5 hrs		Dinner	Dinner	Dinner		Dinner
7		2 hrs	2 hrs	Dance			
8		Break	Break	Pilates	Night Off		2 hrs / Break
9	Yoga	1 hr	1 hr	Break			1 hr
10							

Jane

from............

to............

Weekly Targets:

	Monday	Tuesday	Wednesday	Thursday	Friday	Saturday	Sunday
7		Running		Running		Running	
8			Yoga		Yoga		Yoga
9	ND213 Sports Nutrition	ND 208 Diet Therapy			PD 253 Admin in the NHS	Day Off	
10							
11							
12							
1	Dyslexia						
2				PD 252 Costing & Budgeting	FC 234 Food Processing		
3							
4							
5							
6							
7							
evening							

Figure 1.3   Weekly Planner – Semester 2

	2006								2007												
	September		October		November		December		January		February		March		April		May		June		
Sun			1												1						Sun
Mon			2	W					1	T					2	E					Mon
Tue			3	E					2	I					3	A	1	E			Tue
Wed			4	E	1	E			3	O					4	S	2	E			Wed
Thu			5	K	2	K			4	N	1	K	1	K	5	T	3	K			Thu
Fri	1		6		3		1		5		2		2							E	Fri
Sat	2		7	2	4	6	2	10	6		3	1	3	5	7	R	5	10	2	S	Sat
Sun	3		8		5		3	ND 214 Case Study & Poster	7		4		4		8		6		3	S	Sun
Mon	4		9	W	6	W	4	W	8	W	5	W	5	W	9	V	7	W	4	E	Mon
Tue	5		10	E	7	E	5	E	9	E	6	E	6	E	10	A	8	E	5	X	Tue
Wed	6		11	E	8	E	6	FC 202 Group Report & Presentation	10	E	7	E	7	E	11	C	9	E	6	A	Wed
Thu	7		12	K	9	K	7	ND 211 Group Abstract	11	FC 202 Essay	8	FC 202 Essay	8	FC 202 Essay	12	A	10	FC 202 Essay	7	FC 202 Essay	Thu
Fri	8		13		10		8		12		9		9		13	T	11		8		Fri
Sat	9		14	3	11	7	9	11	13	13	10	2	10	6	14	I	12	11	9		Sat
Sun	10		15		12		10	ND 205 n3/n6	14		11		11		15	O	13		10		Sun
Mon	11		16	W	13	W	11	W	15	E	12	W	12	W	16	N	14	W	11		Mon
Tue	12		17	E	14	E	12	E	16	X	13	E	13	E	17		15	E	12		Tue
Wed	13		18	E	15	E	13	E	17	A	14	E	14	E	18		16	E	13		Wed
Thu	14		19	K	16	K	14	K	18	M	15	K	15	K	19		17	K	14		Thu
Fri	15		20		17		15		19	S	16		16		20		18		15		Fri
Sat	16		21	4	18	8	16	12	20		17	3	17	7	21		19	12	16		Sat
Sun	17		22		19		17	C	21		18		18		22		20		17		Sun
Mon	18		23	W	20	W	18	H	22	E	19	W	19	W	23	W	21	E	18		Mon
Tue	19		24	E	21	ND 211 Practical Report	19	R	23	X	20	E	20	E	24	E	22	X	19		Tue
Wed	20		25	E	22	E	20	I	24	A	21	E	21	E	25	E	23	A	20		Wed
Thu	21		26	K	23	K	21	S	25	M	22	K	22	K	26	K	24	M	21		Thu
Fri	22		27		24		22	T	26	S	23		23		27		25	S	22		Fri
Sat	23		28	5	25	9	23	M	27		24	4	24	8	28	9	26		23		Sat
Sun	24		29		26		24	A	28		25		25		29		27		24		Sun
Mon	25	W	30	W	27	W	25	S	29	W	26	W	26	W	30	W	28	R	25		Mon
Tue	26	E	31	E	28	E	26		30	E	27	E	27	E			29	E	26		Tue
Wed	27	E			29	E	27	V	31	E	28	E	28	E			30	C	27		Wed
Thu	28	K			30	K	28	A					29	K					28		Thu
Fri	29						29	C					30						29		Fri
Sat	30	1					30	A					31	9					30		Sat
Sun							31														Sun

Figure 1.4 Semester or Term Planner – 2006/2007 Academic Year

A 'To do' list

⊙ (GO to To Do List on CD-ROM)

These are very simple to compile and many highly efficient dyslexic and non-dyslexic people use them all the time. All you have to do to compile your list is put down the day or date for the deadline and tick off the tasks as you complete them. Table 1.1 was created in Microsoft Word and can be added to at any time by simply adding rows (see CD-ROM files for Chapter 11).

Table 1.1   To Do List

TO DO	Day	Completed
Group presentation with Sophie and Martin	Thursday 10.00	✓
Collect dinner suit for ball	Friday 5.00	
Buy cat food	asap	

You can adapt all these planning strategies for your own use. Planning enables you to build in enough time for leisure, relaxation and exercise without the worry that you are neglecting your studies. You also should ensure that you have nutritious food and get plenty of sleep.

POINTS TO REMEMBER

This chapter has introduced you to:

- planning and organising your workload;
- planners, weekly timetables and 'To do' lists;
- the importance of balance in your timetable;
- the use of consistent colour codes in your planners.

---

2 Understanding Your Preferred Learning Style

Sandra Hargreaves and Paula Dawson

This chapter:

- gives an overview of the concepts of thinking and learning styles;
- allows you to reflect on how you currently think and learn;
- presents strategies to help you to improve your methods and become a more effective learner;
- provides a learning styles questionnaire to help you find out how you learn best (see link on the CD-ROM);
- explores a range of strategies and techniques associated with the main learning styles – auditory, visual and kinaesthetic.

A lot has been written about **thinking (cognitive)** and **learning** styles and the aim of this chapter is help you find out how you learn most effectively and to try other ways of learning that you may find helpful. Remember you don't have to do everything the same way. As Peri (one of the authors of Chapter 4), has often said, 'I don't make toast the same way I get five dogs in the back of the car'. The key is to make the most of your strengths and minimise your weaknesses.

Thinking styles

Some people know instinctively that they are **holistic** or **analytical** thinkers. If you are a **holistic** thinker, you prefer to think about a **whole** theme, idea or topic before breaking it down into its constituent parts. Another way of describing this way of thinking is '**top down**'. If you are **analytical**, you prefer to conceptualise in smaller, sequential stages building the big picture from the '**bottom up**'. Some tasks are more suited to an overview approach and some require a more systematic sequential approach. For example, making a rough estimate on the basis of approximations is a holistic activity, whereas adding up a column of numbers is an analytical activity.

When discussing approaches to Mathematics (Chapter 8) the terminology changes, describing approaches as those of '**grasshoppers**' referring to holistic thinkers and '**inchworms**' referring to analytical thinkers (Chinn and Ashcroft, 1998).

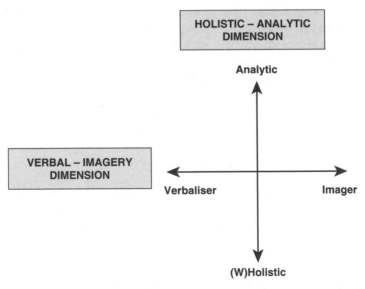

Figure 2.1   Cognitive styles and learning strategies (Riding and Rayner, 1998)

Figure 2.1 can be found in *Cognitive Styles and Learning Strategies* by Riding and Rayner (1998, p. 98). The vertical axis indicates the thinking style spectrum. The more analytical you are (the more you think first of detail), the higher up on this axis you are. Conversely, the more holistic you are (the more you think of the big picture), the lower down you are.

No one is likely to be wholly one or the other. The horizontal axis shows the range of how we think: from thinking in words (verbalising) to thinking in images (visualising). Many people use both thinking processes and comfortably move from one to the other.

You can plot how you think you learn onto this graph. I, for example, know that I am a holistic verbaliser so that I learn best by looking at the whole concept or topic before breaking it into smaller components and I also learn best by articulating my thoughts. Try to plot where you think you lie on this diagram.

Learning styles

So far as learning styles are concerned some students know that they learn better through **visual** methods and that they cannot absorb material when it is only delivered in **auditory** form such as through a lecture or on tape. Others prefer auditory input as they find visual processing difficult. Another group may find that they only learn if they process material while moving, making a model or drawing a plan, which is **kinaesthetic**. There are many overlaps in all these strategies; for example, drawing or creating a concept map is both visual and kinaesthetic. It is also unusual and not good practice for lectures to be totally auditory. Good lecturers include visual elements such as PowerPoint projections and illustrations to break up their delivery. Interactive question and answer sessions and role-play situations involve both auditory and kinaesthetic strategies. There is a wide variety of auditory, visual and kinaesthetic strategies, which are explained in this chapter.

If you feel that you know how you learn best, look at the strategies below, which are suggested under the headings for visual, auditory and kinaesthetic. If not, you might like to do the internet **questionnaire** (see link on the CD-ROM) to see if it helps you to understand what strategies you use. Then you can think about how you might learn more effectively. Note that this link is only one of many different questionnaires attempting to identify learning style.

⊙ **(GO to VARK – A Guide to Learning Styles on CD-ROM)**

Learning strategies

Strategies and techniques are provided in both bullet point format and in a concept map. As you will see from the examples provided below, many of the strategies and techniques do not suit just one learning style, but are in fact multi-sensory.

Visual

There are many strategies a visual learner can employ to aid learning and recall (see Figure 2.2). Visual imagery and association can play an important part. The following list covers many visual strategies:

- Try making up **posters** to display around the room, using pictures to link with words or represent particular aspects of a topic. Use **bright colours** and **colour code** different sections, and use large **font** to make the layout clear and eye-catching.
- **Concept maps** or Mind Maps™ (Buzan) are particularly useful for brainstorming, essay planning, and exam revision. You could draw them onto posters, or use mind-mapping (Buzan) software such as Inspiration, Mind Manager and Mind Genius. (Note: the term Mind Map™ was created by Tony Buzan and the idea has been used in many software programs such as those listed above. For more information see *The Mind Map Book* by Tony Buzan with Barry Buzan, 2006.)
- Use **rooms** in your house for different subjects. For example, in your kitchen, place post-it notes on different appliances and objects to associate them with particular topics. Your **toaster**, **fridge** and **microwave** could all represent different aspects of material you are trying to learn. Then when you are trying to recall the information elsewhere, visualise yourself in your kitchen to trigger your memory.
- Using **visual memory pegs** is another method of recalling information. I have seen this method used very effectively in a wide range of tutorials but it is important to choose your own visual pegs to represent the

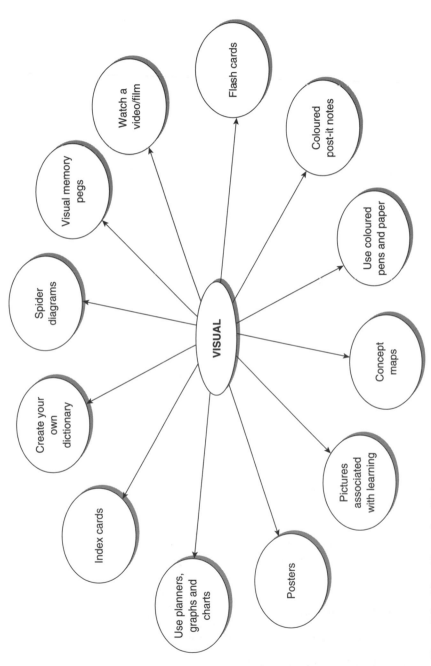

Figure 2.2 Visual Learning Styles

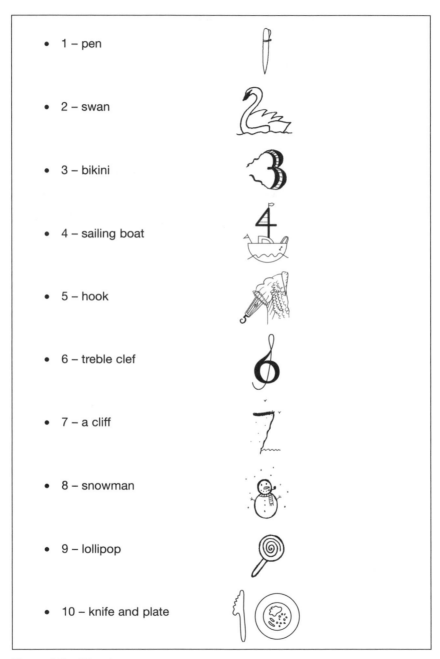

- 1 – pen
- 2 – swan
- 3 – bikini
- 4 – sailing boat
- 5 – hook
- 6 – treble clef
- 7 – a cliff
- 8 – snowman
- 9 – lollipop
- 10 – knife and plate

Figure 2.3   Visual memory pegs

numbers in the list so that you can recall them easily and link them effectively to what you are trying to learn. The original idea for this can be found in Buzan (1988) *Make the Most of Your Mind*, but has been adapted to suit personal visual cues. Figure 2.3 shows how the numbers from 1–10 can be linked to a visual image, which looks like the number. These visual images can then be linked to whatever you are trying to recall.

- When **revising** for exams, you could write questions with answers on the back of **index cards**. It is a good idea to **colour code** your index cards so that you have different coloured cards for each subject or topic (see Chapter 9, 'Examination Techniques').

- **Planners** or **wall charts** are visual and are a good way of organising and planning your workload (see Chapter 1, 'Managing Your Workload'). Enter onto them all your coursework deadlines and examination dates, as well as any important social events or activities. Monthly, semester or even yearly planners allow you to have an overview of important deadlines and events, allowing you to plan in advance. Weekly planners can help you to organise your workload on a day-to-day basis. Use a different coloured **highlighter** pen for each subject, or regular activity, such as a yoga class. Planners can be enlarged and put onto your wall to jog your memory, help you keep on task and to keep appointments on time. They can also be used as screen savers.

Auditory

There are many strategies an auditory learner can employ to aid learning and recall (see Figure 2.4). **Sound imagery** and **association** can play an important part. The following list covers many auditory strategies:

- **Mnemonics** are auditory devises, such or rhymes or catchy phrases, which act as important aids to recall information such as factual terms and material or even how to spell a word. An example of this is the phrase 'there is a **rat** in sepa**rat**e', to remind you how to spell this word. Many music students remember the notes, which represent the lines and spaces of the treble and bass clefs, through mnemonics. The notes **EGBDF**, which represent the lines of the treble clef, are usually remembered with the mnemonic: **E**very **G**ood **B**oy **D**eserves **F**ruit.

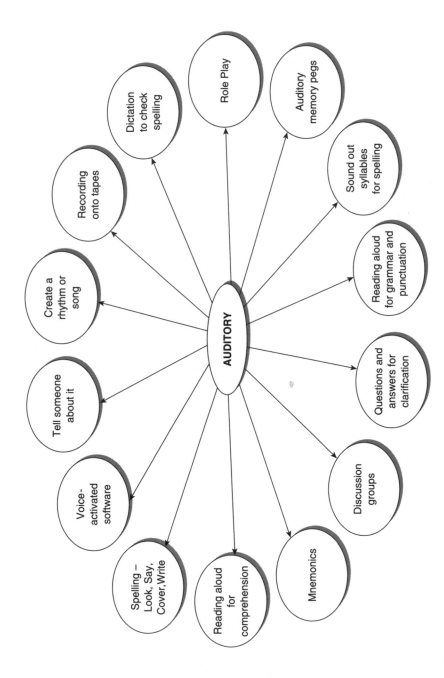

Figure 2.4 Auditory learning styles

- **Acronyms** are very common auditory devices which use the first letter of each key word to make a new word, for example: **WHO** for **W**orld **H**ealth **O**rganization and **UNESCO** for **U**nited **N**ations **E**ducational, **S**cientific and **C**ultural **O**rganization. Many of these have become so embedded in the structure of the language that they have become words in their own right. You can use this technique to help you remember information for examinations, as you will see in Chapter 9, 'Examination Techniques'. The word doesn't have to be a real word; it can be something which you have made up – which may even make it more memorable to you. Applying a rhythm or a beat to it can also help you to remember it.
- Sound imagery and association are used in **auditory memory pegs** for those who prefer to learn by auditory methods. This very useful memory device is set out in Tony Buzan's excellent book on memory, *Use Your Head* (1995). The auditory memory pegs are based on the old English rhyme *This Old Man* and each number in the rhyme is **linked to a word which sounds like the number**. The old rhyme goes:

  This old man, he played one, he played knick-knack on my drum ...

  and continues through all the numbers: **two/shoe**, **three/knee**, **four/door**, **five/hive**, **six/sticks**, **seven/heaven**, **eight/gate**, **nine/line** and **ten/hen**. As with the visual pegs it is important to know these auditory pegs well, and to be able to recall them immediately. Thus when you have linked them in memory with whatever information you are trying to remember, your recall of the information will be improved. (For further information on this technique with excellent illustrations, see *Use Your Head* by Tony Buzan.)
- Try **reading your work aloud**, or getting someone else to read it aloud for you. Many people find that by using this technique, they are able to hear how their work sounds, in order to spot any mistakes and then make corrections. Mistakes are often difficult to spot when you have read it over many times to yourself. Reading aloud also allows you to check your punctuation. This way you can pick up on natural pauses where it may be necessary to add commas or full stops.
- **Software programs** such as TextHELP Read & Write, ClaroRead and Kurzweil will also read back your work to you. If you are having trouble

reading difficult text or challenging articles, you can also scan in pages of text or articles, which can be read back to you using the software (see Chapter 11, 'How ICT Can Help You').

- If you have difficulty word processing but no difficulty articulating your ideas, you might benefit from using another software program, Dragon Naturally Speaking, and other similar packages, which **convert your speech into text** files. This software needs to be trained but is used widely by both dyslexic and non-dyslexic people who find it very helpful to write essays, reports and emails.
- If you find it difficult to take notes in lectures, and often find that you are not able to take down enough information, you could try using a mini-disk recorder or other recording device **to record your lectures so that you can listen to them later** at home at your own pace. All you need to do during the lecture is write down the number on the elapsed time counter at significant points in the lecture. Then at home, and as soon as possible, use the counter to fast forward to selected sections and **make notes on the content** (see Chapter 3). The actual recording can be used for revision but be aware this could become time consuming. Be selective!
- A useful way of developing your understanding of a subject or concept is to **talk it over with someone**. You could get together with a classmate and discuss ideas with them, which of course will help them too. If you are unsure of what an essay question is asking you to do, discuss what your understanding is of the question with your lecturer or module tutor so that you can ensure you are on the right track.

Kinaesthetic

Some kinaesthetic learners find they study best while **moving, listening** to music, or **chewing** gum or **eating** something. Further suggestions are provided in Figure 2.5 and below.

- You could compile **study notes** on a mini-disk and listen to them while going for a walk or a jog.
- If you are revising for exams, you may find it helpful to write out your notes a few times, condensing them down to just a few **key words** that

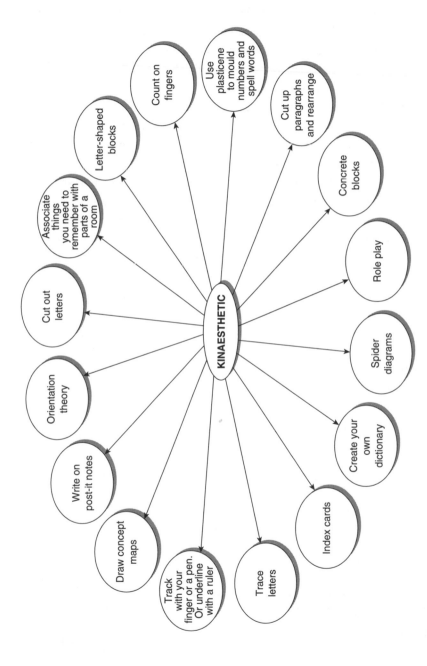

Figure 2.5   Kinaesthetic learning styles

will trigger your memory of the subject. You could use highlighter pens to colour code different topics, or draw pictures to relate to the different topics (see Chapter 9, 'Examination Techniques').

- If you enjoy a hands-on approach, you may like to experiment with plastic letters or modelling letters in clay to learn words and letters you find difficult. An effective multi-sensory spelling strategy is the **Look, Say, Cover, Write, and Check** method, which is covered in Chapter 7.

- If you have a presentation to do, **practise your presentation** in front of someone you know, in the mirror or on video. This will help to build your confidence and will allow you to check that you have got the timing right. If the presentation is meant to be for 15 minutes, make sure it is no longer and don't bore your audience by running over time. PowerPoint is a very useful tool for presentations for both dyslexic and non-dyslexic students as it helps you to speak articulately with prompts from the screen, which you can move on with simple key-strokes. The other wonderful thing is that if you are nervous, the PowerPoint slides direct the audience's attention away from you to the screen.

- **Role play** is an effective way of putting your knowledge into practice. If you are training to be a nurse or teacher, for example, try role playing a consultation with a patient, or an interview with a parent (see Chapter 10, 'Using Role Play' for further ideas).

CASE STUDY

Doris, a psychology student, found this type of visual/kinaesthetic approach helpful because she could visualise all the ideas and issues involved before moving on to the outline of the essay and the essay itself (see Chapter 5, 'Answering Essay Questions').

Essay concept map

The key to this concept map is organisation by colour. By isolating the issues that need to be addressed in the brief in different colours I was able

(Continued)

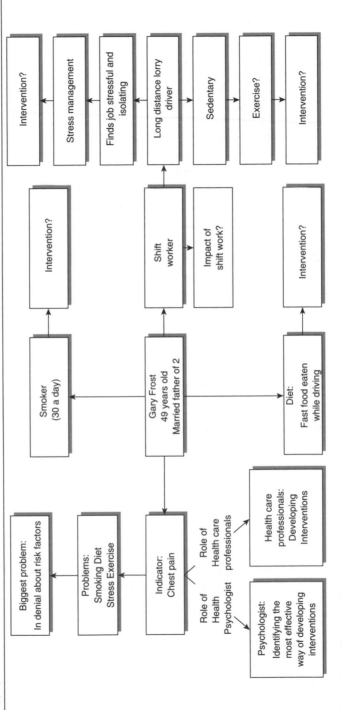

Case study concept map

Gary Frost is a 49-year-old married father of two, who has worked shifts as a long distance lorry driver for the past twenty years. He spends most of his time in his cab, travelling across England. He finds his job isolating and quite stressful at times. He often becomes agitated and restless, feeling hostile towards other drivers on the road when spending long periods of time sitting in traffic on the motorway. He eats mainly fast, fatty foods whilst he is on the road and finds little time to exercise. Mr Frost smokes thirty cigarettes a day and has recently suffered with chest pains. His wife is becoming increasingly more worried about his health, but Mr Frost thinks that his wife is worrying over nothing and that his recent chest pains are simply a result of indigestion caused by eating and driving simultaneously.

Identify and refine problems or issues related to this case. Identify the roles of a health psychologist and other health care professionals dealing with this case. Develop an appropriate treatment/intervention plan

Intervention?

Stress management

Finds job stressful and isolating

Long distance lorry driver

Sedentary

Exercise?

Intervention?

Intervention?

Shift worker

Impact of shift work?

Smoker (30 a day)

Gary Frost 49 years old Married father of 2

Diet: Fast food eaten while driving

Intervention?

Biggest problem: In denial about risk factors

Problems: Smoking Diet Stress Exercise

Indicator: Chest pain

Role of Health care professionals

Health care professionals: Developing Interventions

Role of Health Psychologist

Psychologist: Identifying the most effective way of developing interventions

Figure 2.6   Case study concept map

(Continued)

to see at a glance what I needed to cover and how the various issues were linked. The concept map also gave me the structure for the essay. The left of the concept map (the issues not related to an intervention) formed the basis of my introduction and how I was going to address the question. This delineated how I conceived the issues and the agencies I thought should be involved in the intervention. On the right-hand side of the concept map are those issues that are related to the proposed intervention. As you can see the issue of shift work is mentioned but no intervention is proposed. This is part of the job description and not possible to change; my reading, however, indicted that it was a significant risk factor and therefore should be mentioned in the write-up.

The concept map shown in Figure. 2.6 was produced by Doris in response to an essay question on vocational health issues.

POINTS TO REMEMBER

- Understand your thinking style (holistic or analytical) and your learning style (visual, auditory, kinaesthetic or multi-sensory).
- Try to use your own cognitive and learning styles to develop techniques that will help you.
- Be prepared to use multi-sensory methods and different methods for different purposes.
- Use materials or software that appeal to your own needs and be prepared to adapt them if necessary.
- Don't be surprised if you prefer to work in a range of methods and techniques – try them and use what is successful.
- Be prepared to seek or ask for more expert help if this is appropriate.

3 Note Taking and Note Making

Kay McEachran

This chapter:

- considers the difficulties of note taking and note making;
- illustrates the importance and purpose of good notes;
- considers the role of learning style;
- looks at various strategies for compiling notes;
- analyses different systems for taking and making notes;
- shows you how to make use of appropriate technology;
- provides useful templates for note taking and note making.

Difficulties

Note taking and note making at college or university can be especially difficult for dyslexic students, as both activities require you to perform a number of different tasks at once, some of which you may have difficulty with. These can include: listening comprehension; reading comprehension; information processing; organisation, flow and structuring of work; clarity of writing; and writing speed.

One area you may have particular difficulty with is knowing exactly what information to write down and what to leave out, which can result in you either desperately trying to note everything down or giving up entirely. **You don't need to write down everything that is said in a lecture**. If, for example, a lecturer tells a joke or an amusing anecdote, you must ask yourself if it is crucial to your understanding of the topic being discussed; if it isn't, then disregard it.

Identifying **key points** and the organisation and structure of notes can be problematic. Here, you can either take the lead from your lecturer, or the author if you are making notes from text. They will have done the bulk of the work for you – especially if your lecturer provides handouts. Headings and subheadings indicate key points and they will more than likely be given in a logical sequence. So make the most of the work already done for you.

You will not be the only student who is daunted by the prospect of taking or making notes. By introducing and practising useful strategies your notes will improve, hopefully making the process easier.

Differences between note taking and note making

Generally speaking, **note taking involves taking notes from speech** (e.g. lectures, videos, audio tape, and dictation) where there is less control of the process and usually more pressure due to time restrictions. Even when this exercise involves copying from a board or overhead projector, there tends to be a time limit.

Note making (usually from text or rewriting notes) is not subject to the same time constraints. Students often feel that they have more control when they are making notes and therefore tend to feel less pressured by this activity. Making notes enables you to reorganise your thoughts and ideas, and put them into your own words, rather than your lecturer's, and hopefully remember them better because of this.

The importance of good notes

This should not be underestimated. Your academic success will undoubtedly depend on the quality of your notes, as they will form the basis of your exam revision and essays or assignments. It is vitally important that you approach your note taking and note making seriously from the very beginning of your course. Try not to fall behind – you may not have time to catch up later on.

Good notes can be one of the most important resources for all students for both assignment preparation and examination revision. To appreciate this fact you will have to identify your reasons for taking/making them (their purpose), as well as their functions.

Why take or make notes?

- To engage/interact with the material being studied.
- To assist in writing essays and assignments.
- To formulate ideas.
- To remember and make sense of material.
- For revision purposes.
- For reviewing or reformulating ideas.

The importance of identifying learning style

The value of identifying your learning style lies in **helping you identify your strengths and weaknesses**, and might therefore encourage you to concentrate on using strategies which complement your areas of strength when compiling notes.

If you are a **visual learner**, you may have a preference for concept maps (for holistic thinkers) and linear notes (for analytical thinkers). You might also like to compile wall charts or diagrams and use colour. If you are an **auditory learner**, you may prefer to record lectures and/ or yourself talking about the lecture afterwards. Other auditory approaches would be to discuss the lecture topic with friends or listen for **clues** and **signal words** during the lecture. Examples of these would be: 'an important theory is', 'the main points are', or statements like 'next we will consider'. **Kinaesthetic learners** prefer active learning and might like to use a combination of the methods above.

Listed below are a number of general strategies for note taking and note making, many of which are **multi-sensory** (i.e. appeal to all learning styles). It should be stressed, however, that these are only guidelines and that you should be flexible and use whichever strategies you feel comfortable with, regardless of your learning style.

Don't limit yourself to learning methods considered suitable for your learning style. Mix and match strategies to suit yourself. Chances are, you will know which methods work best for you anyway. **If one method is not working for you, try another**.

General strategies for note taking and note making

- Prepare in advance if possible and familiarise yourself with the topic. Keep ahead of your required reading by asking for a prioritised reading list which indicates the essential source material. This may help to ensure that you have more idea of those points which are worth noting down, and those which aren't, thereby giving you more time to listen. **Lectures will make more sense if you already have a general idea of what the lecturer is talking about**.
- Be **punctual and ready to take notes from the very beginning** of the lecture. This is when most lecturers will **provide signposts and key points**. Use these – if your lecturer has taken the trouble to mention them, they will be important.
- Listen to your lecturer's **summing up at the end of a lecture**, to ensure you have included all the points listed.
- Jot down **key words and phrases**.
- **Always attend class, if you can**. Second-hand notes are difficult to decipher. By all means use another student's notes in addition to your own, but you still need the gist of the lecture in order for them to be useful. Only use another's notes as a last resort.

- Use **a large loose-leaf notebook** (a different one for each module/subject). This way you can easily insert extra pages or remove pages in future.
- Write the **date and title at the top of the first page** – it makes filing easier.
- **Only write on one side of the paper**, double space the lines, and leave plenty of space (for adding points later).
- Write **source references and page numbers** in the margin.
- Follow the **book or chapter order** when making notes from text. This will ensure your notes follow a logical sequence.
- Leave out unnecessary words (such as the, a, an).
- Use **shorthand, abbreviations or symbols**, particularly for words common to your subject. You can design your own (the more personal the better).
- Use thought plans or Mind Maps™ as this may help you link ideas and concepts.
- Indicate the words you don't understand or have difficulty in spelling by highlighting them or writing them in a different colour. You could even just write them in **bold**, BLOCK CAPITALS or in larger print if you find this quicker or you don't have any colours with you.
- Have a **dictionary to hand** when making notes or rewriting notes, to check any unfamiliar words. **Do not do this when taking notes** – you will not have time!
- Copy the **information provided on boards or overheads**, as they will contain the points that your lecturer considers to be important. (Remember, they know what is necessary to pass your course!)
- Sit next to a good note taker – near point copying is often easier than copying from a board or overheads. (Remember, copying notes is not cheating, but do ask first!)
- Ask your lecturer to provide copies of **overheads and handouts** before the start of the lecture. If they are available electronically, download them in advance. This way you may only need to make additional notes or examples.
- **Record lectures** if you have difficulty taking notes, but remember to ask your lecturer. Auditory learners may find this a useful supplement to the notes they take in class (see Chapter 2).
- If your **keyboard skills are better** than your handwriting skills, **take a laptop to lectures**, or use a small keyboard and download onto your computer later. Always check beforehand if this is permissible.

- Write up notes as soon as possible after the lecture.
- Talk about the lecture afterwards.

Not all of these strategies will be suitable for you. **Only use those that work for you in conjunction with one or more of the suggested techniques for compiling notes** (see below) in order for your notes to be as effective as possible.

Suggested note-taking and note-making methods

The Two Column Method (Cornell system)

(∘) **(GO to Two Column (Cornell) Template and Example on CD-ROM)**

This double entry system is considered particularly suitable for dyslexic students for two reasons:

- it applies to both note taking and note making;
- it is a **multi-sensory** technique requiring you **to record, reduce, recite, reflect on, and review** your notes.

The method follows three basic steps:

Step 1   Before the lecture draw a vertical line 6 cm from the left-hand side of your page. This is the **recall column**. To the right of this margin is the **note-taking column**.

Step 2   During the lecture record notes in the main column as fully and clearly as you can. Use abbreviations – it will save time. Skip lines. You can do this for a number of reasons:

- To show the end of particular ideas or thoughts
- If you lose your train of thought
- You cannot keep up with the lecturer
- You don't fully understand what is being said.

In each case, mark the gap with a symbol or word to identify the reason for the blank space. Using words such as 'END' or a question mark will help.

Step 3 After the lecture **reduce** your notes by jotting down ideas and **key words** (cues) in the recall column (use drawings and symbols if you prefer). These should immediately give you the idea of the lecture. This process should help clarify the meaning and relationships of ideas.

Next, **recite** the main facts and ideas of the lecture by covering the main column, and only using the cues in the recall column. This process helps commit facts and ideas to your long-term memory. At this stage you may also begin to **reflect** and come up with new ideas and relationships.

Finally, a quick **review** of the key words in your recall columns for a few minutes each week will help you remember much of what you have made notes on.

This method has many similarities to the SQ3R Reading Strategy discussed in Chapter 4.

Advantages ✔	Interactive and extremely efficient once mastered – helps avoid rewriting notes.
Disadvantages ✗	You may need time and practice to get the hang of this method.

ⓞ Q Notes (Question and Answer Notes)

ⓞ (GO to Q Notes Template and Example on CD-ROM)

The originator (Jim Burke, www.englishcompanion.com) of this note-making system calls it Q Notes, because it requires that you make up Q-uestions (left-hand column), and Q-uiz yourself (right-hand answer column). **This process will no doubt be easier if you originally used the two-column method to compile your notes**.

For revision purposes cover up the answer column and look at the questions – these act as cues to remind you of what you should know.

Advantages ✔	An excellent revision aid.
Disadvantages ✘	As with the two-column method it may require practice.

Four Quarter Method

(GO to Four Quarter System Template and Example on CD-ROM)

You might find that dividing a page into 4 quarters helps with your note taking. Each of the quarters represents 15 minutes of an hour-long lecture (if your lecture is longer, say 2 hours, then you could divide up 2 pages).

Psychologically and visually this is a satisfying method, since you are always aware of just how far into a lecture you are. In addition, as space is limited, it encourages the use of **key words** and abbreviations. It is also a useful technique if you are recording a lecture, and do not have a counter on your recording device, as you will see at a glance which section/s of the lecture you have missed and should replay.

Advantages ✔	Encourages interactive note taking.
Disadvantages ✘	You will need to be very concise.

Linear

This method uses **subheadings, key points and lists** to highlight points. It may appeal more to visual learners. Figure 3.1 is an example of what brief linear revision notes on this chapter might look like, using a variety of these methods.

(⊙) **(GO to Linear Notes Example on CD-ROM)**

Advantages ✔	May help keep you focused during lectures and keep with the flow of a lecture or argument. Can save you rewriting notes.
Disadvantages ✗	Very laborious. Can result in unnecessary material which you may be tempted to use simply because you have written it down. Only helps avoid rewriting notes if you are an efficient note taker in the first place. To be avoided if your handwriting speed is slow.

Concept maps (thought plans and spider diagrams)

Concept maps (as shown in Figure 3.2) begin with the main point/central theme written or drawn in the centre of the page. From this central idea or image a pattern of ideas are added via a series of connecting lines. These can represent ideas, themes, arguments, examples or relationships between ideas (e.g. cause and effect). These cross-links and cross-references are easy to add and the expansion of ideas just continues outwards. Examples of Mind Maps™ can be found in Chapters 2 and 5.

By the nature of their design, concept maps can include **colours, drawings and symbols.** By using these maps, you can fit a whole lecture or topic onto one page (it is best to turn the paper horizontally).

Taking/Making notes

Difficulties
Need to perform no. of different processes at once
Knowing what to include – use handouts (identify **key points**, use **headings**, **subheadings**, etc.)

Differences
Note taking   →   speech
Note making   →   text & rewriting

Importance
V. important!
Exams
Essays

Learning Styles
Visual ?
Auditory?   }   BE FLEXIBLE! ! !
Kinaesthetic?

Strategies

List:

1 Prepare in advance
2 Punctuality

Methods
Again list:

Two Column Method
Q Notes
Four Quarter Method
Linear
Concept maps

Use of technology
• Recording devices
• Laptops

Figure 3.1   An example of linear notes based on the chapter

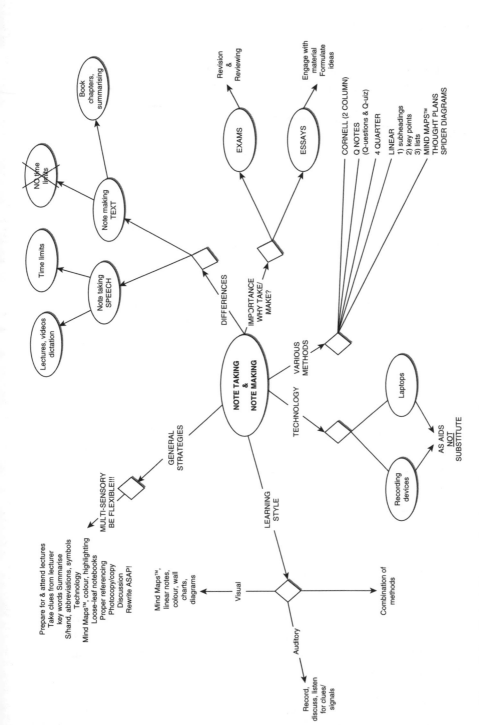

Figure 3.2   Note-taking and note-making concept map

Concept maps can be constructed by using pens and paper or by using software programs such as Inspiration or Mind Manager (see Chapter 11, 'How ICT Can Help You').

You might prefer using concept maps during lectures and converting them into more conventional linear notes afterwards.

Advantages ✔	Fewer words used. Useful if your handwriting speed is slow. They help organise and condense material.
Disadvantages ✗	Can be confusing and may require a certain amount of training. Must be organised systematically and consistently. More useful when making notes than taking notes.

Think of rewriting notes or converting them into concept maps or patterned notes as useful revision time. **Any activity that involves reprocessing notes improves recall** and therefore acts as a form of revision. In addition, you will be left with a set of understandable reusable notes for the future!

Use of technology

The use of recording devices and laptops for compiling notes has already been mentioned above, and the use of information and communications technology (ICT) will be covered in Chapter 11. There are, however, some general points to be made and **advantages** and **potential pitfalls** to consider.

Recording notes

- Use **a recorder with a counting device**. If at some point you lose track, simply **make a note of the number on the counter**, then after the lecture you merely have to locate this number on the counter rather than listen to the whole lecture again.
- **Record yourself talking about a subject**. This encourages the creative flow of ideas without the worry of having to write them down simultaneously – there will be time for that afterwards.
- **Label and date your recorded notes** in order to avoid confusion and make them easier to find.
- **Write up recordings as soon as possible** after lectures while they are still fresh in your mind. Be selective (see Chapter 2).

Advantages ✔	Very useful for students with an auditory preference, and/or a slow handwriting speed.
Potential pitfalls ✗	Try only to use this method as a back-up, as you may become a passive rather than an attentive listener and/or end up with a backlog of recordings. Remember, compiling notes should be an **interactive experience**.

Using laptops

Taking a laptop into lectures can be very useful if you have good keyboard skills. If you can touch type, then you will be able to concentrate on the board, or overheads without having to keep looking down at what you are writing. Small keyboards, such as an AlphaSmart (see Chapter 11) are also useful as they are light and portable and you can download from them onto your computer.

Advantages ✔	Your notes will be legible, and easy to expand upon at some point in the future, thus saving time. You are able to use the spellchecker or thesaurus on your PC.
Potential pitfalls ✗	Don't neglect your handwriting skills. Always ask permission to use a keyboard. Don't take your spellchecker for granted – they are useful, but not infallible.

Technology should be used as an aid when compiling notes, **but never as a substitute** for your own notes.

CASE STUDY

Atif had a written test, which was unusual for his course as most of it was based on course work, much of it practical.

He worked on making revision notes. He knew which topics were likely to come up in the test, but his lecture notes weren't really up to scratch. He did have his course handouts, however, which we worked through to make notes on each of the major topics. He used the headings and subheadings as signposts.

He had a visual preference, and by using a combination of drawings, colour, illustrations, Mind Maps™ and abbreviations he managed to fit each topic onto a single page. As well as now having notes for future use, the physical act of converting the lecture notes into an understandable and usable format caused him to review his notes and therefore acted as revision.

He passed his test with a very good mark. He explained that once he had converted his course handouts into his own words and drawings the test was psychologically less of a challenge. It had seemed 'a much smaller hill to climb'. He was also less afraid of written tests in the future.

POINTS TO REMEMBER

This chapter has introduced you to:

- the importance of good note taking/making;
- overall strategies to help with note taking and note making;
- various note-taking and note-making methods;
- the role of technology in compiling notes.

Remember – the beauty of taking or making notes is that you only have to please yourself. All that matters is that **your notes make sense to you**. Marks are not gained for the notes themselves, but rather your ability to **utilise them for revision or coursework**.

4 Reading Strategies and Speed Reading

Peri Batliwala and Judith Cattermole

This chapter aims to help you:

- understand your present reading habits;
- use your library;
- apply an efficient reading strategy to your reading;
- understand how comprehension can be enhanced;
- understand how reading speed can be improved.

Reading at college or university

It is obvious but necessary to state that one of the greatest demands of college or university life for any student is the reading load, in terms of both quantity and complexity. There is some variation, depending on the course chosen, but it is fair to say that if you can't read efficiently and with reasonable fluency, you will feel over-whelmed and under-equipped for all the tasks required of you: under-taking research, writing essays, understanding lectures, and ultimately, sitting exams.

It is critical therefore that you, as an adult dyslexic student with reading difficulties, seek help with **prioritising texts on reading lists**, by asking your tutors which are the most essential texts and **learning any strategies that make it possible for you to read efficiently and with good understanding**.

Reading and dyslexia

It is fairly generally agreed that reading weakness is a fairly reliable sign of the 'distinctive balance of skills', as Gilroy and Miles characterise dyslexia (1996, p. 1). Indeed it is reading weakness which gives rise to the 'discrepancy definition' of dyslexia when there is a marked discrepancy between a reading score and age/IQ. In other words **reading is probably harder for you than for non-dyslexic students**.

It is very important to set aside **specific time slots** for reading in your weekly schedule (see Chapter 1) and to stick to them. This will help in two ways. First, it will keep you on schedule and avoid the temptation of 'doing it later'. Secondly, it will stop you reading for longer than you have allocated in a particular subject area. Most dyslexic students report that they 'sit for hours reading and that nothing goes in'. You need to avoid this and can do so by **adopting a reading strategy** and by **changing your activity** when you are **losing concentration**. Break up your reading into chunks of 30- or 45-minute slots. If you are losing concentration even with a reading strategy, use shorter slots. It is important to use your time effectively and eliminate the feeling of despair which arises when you have spent hours in the library and feel you have learnt little.

Using a library

The library is an important source of help as it provides information and services as well as books, journals and other materials. It is important for you as a dyslexic student to take some time to explore the library before you need to start using it.

Start finding out about your library:

- By visiting and walking round. **Get to know where different things are located** before you need to find the materials you require. Often dyslexic students find it difficult to work in open plan spaces so ask if there are any small, quiet rooms or study carrels (individual desks with sides) that you can use to study in to avoid distractions. Take time to try out different desks or tables and choose the ones that suit you best. Sometimes the library can get very busy so if this bothers you, **try to visit at quieter times** and when staff will have more time to help you.

- By visiting the library website. This will give you a summary of all the services on offer and probably a list of the names and contact details of staff who can help you.
- By contacting key members of the library staff. Some libraries have staff who have a special responsibility for helping students with dyslexia and other disabilities.

To help you use the library efficiently you will need to find answers to the following questions:

- How do you join the library?
- How many items can you borrow?
- What sort of library materials can you not take out? These are usually called reference materials and often include journals.
- Can you reserve books and how do you collect them?
- Are there any **special arrangements for dyslexic students**? These can include being allowed to borrow items for longer or not having to pay fines. Each library is different and sometimes issue dyslexic students with a special card.
- Can you renew or make reservations online or by phone?
- Can you use your own laptop in the library?

The main types of materials you will find in a library are:

- Books: these are usually arranged on the shelves by subject. Each book is given a reference or class number. You can find this number by using the library catalogue. To do this **you will need to know either the author or title or subject. Make sure you have the correct spelling!** Most catalogues are computerised and the library will have terminals you can use as well as being able to access the catalogue online remotely, e.g. from home or where you work. Some class numbers can be long (often ten or more digits) so make sure you have pen and paper with you to write down the number before you go to the shelves.

- Journals or periodicals or magazines and newspapers: these are usually shelved alphabetically by title. Remember that if a title starts with the word 'The', you must ignore it when looking on the shelves. So: *The Labour Law Journal* would be in the 'L' section of the journals.
- Abstracts and indexes: these give brief details of journal articles. They may look difficult to use but are in fact quite easy although you may need to ask for some help to start you off.
- Electronic information: a lot of the material including journals and abstracts and indexes you will need to use is now available electronically. To access some specialist academic material you may need a password, often called an Athens password.

Using a reading strategy

The basic concept behind all reading strategies is that you should **read with a purpose** so that your mind does not wander, and so that all the time you are reading you are on task and no time is wasted. They all employ three different types of reading – namely, **skimming, scanning and reading for meaning**. **Skimming** requires you to look quickly over a piece of text to check for the main features; **scanning** requires you to look for something specific such as an answer to a question; while **reading for meaning** requires reading directed towards comprehending the text.

Some of the reliable and well-known strategies are:

- **SQ3R** (Survey, Question, Read, Recall, and Review)
  (cited in Ott, 1997, p. 182)
- **PASS** (Preview, Ask and Answer Questions, Summarise and Synthesise)
  (cited in McLoughlin, Leather and Stringer, 2003, p. 137).

To help you try one or more of these strategies we will look at the most well-known of these strategies, SQ3R, in more detail. The stages of the **SQ3R Method** are:

Survey	Look over the section or paragraph you are reading. This requires you to **skim read** to determine the length of the piece

	and if there are any subheadings or topic sentences you can then use for the next stage.
Question	If there are **subheadings** in the text, turn them into **questions** to give you a purpose for your reading. If there are no subheadings, look at the first sentence of each paragraph to see if it is a **topic sentence**. Change this into a question so that you can read the remainder of the paragraph to find the answer.
Read	This requires you to **read for meaning** so that you can answer the question you have raised in the previous step.
Recall	This stage ensures that you have understood the text you have read and can recall the information to answer the question you have raised. This may require you to **scan the text** for information such as a date or name.
Review	This final stage requires you to think about the information you have read and **to reflect** on whether you agree with it and whether it fits in with other reading you have done on the subject.

Additionally, there are often clues to content in the structure of many paragraphs. Therefore, it may be a good idea to focus on and absorb the topic sentence and concluding sentence of a paragraph, and develop a 'recognition span' for key words and phrases (Gilroy and Miles, 1996, p. 86).

(◦) **(GO to SQ3R Reading Comprehension on CD-ROM)**

PASS differs slightly from SQ3R. **Preview**, **Ask** and **Answer Questions** are similar to Survey, Question and Read, but with greater emphasis on answering questions as you read. The **Summarise** stage is Recall with note making (Chapter 3) and **Synthesise** implies reducing material as you analyse it and make notes.

Again whichever strategy you choose, the important thing is that you are **actively engaging with the material** to take what you need from it. **This puts you in control of your reading**.

Scotopic sensitivity (meares-irlen syndrome)

This is a condition which affects some dyslexic students. If you have difficulty reading black typeface on white background, or you see 'rivers of white' running down the page, or the words become jumbled, you may have Scotopic Sensitivity. Although you can follow this up with a formal assessment which will determine the colours that suit you, you can help yourself at very little cost. Go to a stationery shop and **try out some different coloured plastic folders**. Put in some black text on white paper and see which colour improves your ability to read and reduces your visual discomfort. You can use the same coloured background on your PC monitor (see Chapter 11).

Quite often Scotopic Sensitivity assessments are funded by the Local Authorities (LAs) as part of the Disabled Students' Allowance (DSA). For more information about the condition visit the Institute of Optometry website:

www.ioo.org.uk/dyslexia.htm

Reading can be more difficult if the text is dense, full of jargon or abbreviations, and if it is poorly laid out. This could be due a serif font (one with loops at the top and bottom of letters), small font size, poor spacing and right justification. Use a dictionary and thesaurus to clarify the words that are impeding your reading progress (see Chapter 11 for electronic dictionaries and thesaurus). The problems associated with layout can be rectified either by **photocopying and enlarging the text** and using coloured folders, or by **scanning the text into your computer**, and changing the font size and background to your preferred colours.

Ideal conditions for reading

Reading is easier if you are sitting in a comfortable, well-lit environment. Good posture optimises reading and comprehension. Sitting upright enables the brain to receive the maximum flow of air and blood, and means that lower back pain and shoulder aches are relieved. The brain 'sits up and pays attention' because the body is alert. Your eyes can make full use of their peripheral vision. Sit at a table in a relaxed, upright posture with the book on the table in front of you at a distance of about 50 cm.

What is comprehension?

To put it simply, there would be no point in reading if we didn't understand what the words meant.

To put it more technically, comprehension,

> when applied to **reading is an ability to understand and recall the contents of what has been read**. It requires fluent decoding skills (reading with automaticity), knowledge of word meanings and an ability to use previous experience or contextual cues to understand the meaning which is being conveyed by the words. (Ott, 1997, p. 376; emphasis added)

So if you can read faster, it doesn't mean that you will find it harder to understand what you are reading. On the contrary, dyslexia experts maintain that, 'being able to read quickly is … important to comprehension. Unless a person can read at a good rate they cannot keep the content in memory long enough to comprehend it' (McLoughlin *et al.*, 2003, p. 62).

Efficient comprehension is the whole point of reading. At college or university, in the workplace, for practical purposes or for pleasurable good reading, **comprehension is the key skill**.

To spell it out, 'if one were to choose a particular aspect of reading which would predict success in an occupation it would be silent reading comprehension' (McLoughlin *et al.*, 2003, p. 6).

The sort of comprehension required of you at college or university is **critical thinking**, i.e. making connections, identifying relevance, fitting new information into an existing framework or putting into context. It is not merely a matter of literal questioning which is reliant on short-term memory (like so many of the assessment methods in popular speed-reading books) but it is based more on inferential comprehension where you are expected to make connections, draw inferences, interpret, question and critically analyse a written text.

Speed reading

So if you think that your reading speed hinders your comprehension and could be improved, try some of the following techniques with a reading strategy. If you are too busy during term time, maybe try them in the holidays.

As a result of your diagnosis for dyslexia, you should be aware of your current reading speed. If not, it is worth asking your dyslexia co-ordinator for a reading test. You can do a rough reading test for yourself by reading an unfamiliar passage for 1 minute, then counting how many words you read. Or try the test on the internet. The average speed for college/university students is between 200 and 250 words per minute (wpm).

www.rocketreader.com/cgi-bin/portal/fun_tests/perception

What is important for you to know is that, whatever your speed, it can be improved with a combination of improved reading techniques to help you read faster, and a strategy to help you read more actively (i.e. knowing what it is you want from the text).

Techniques you can use to read faster

Theory 1   The eyes read by a series of jumps (saccades) and fixations (pauses) along the line of text. Fixations are the only times at which information is absorbed. These fixations can take between ¼ and 1½ seconds. Poor readers make frequent, longer fixations, fast readers fewer, shorter ones. Although we may have been told to read 'slowly and carefully' in the past, in the belief that we would understand more, in fact the opposite is true.

Technique   By **limiting the number of fixations** and making them quicker than usual, your eyes will move over the text more fluently, and with increased comprehension.

Theory 2   Poor readers read one word at a time. Actually our peripheral vision enables us to take in groups of words up to 5–7 at a time, and to grasp the sense of the sentence.

Technique   **Move your eyes forward quickly, consciously forcing yourself to skim read words in clusters**.

Theory 3   Poor readers often back-skip or regress because they haven't understood a word, or feel they have missed something, or because their attention has wandered. Regression means more fixations and more wasted time.

Technique   Consciously determine to **only move your eyes forward quickly**, to keep your attention on the page, and trust to your word knowledge and context to 'make up' for a word that you may have missed or not understood.

Theory 4   The eyes move more smoothly and efficiently if they are guided by a slim implement such as a pencil, chopstick or knitting needle. Moving your finger from word to word, on the other hand, slows down the reading while your hand on the page blocks your peripheral awareness of the surrounding text.

Technique   **Run a pencil or chopstick quickly and smoothly along the text** to guide your eyes forward line by line. Eventually just passing the pencil/chopstick down the page in a flowing movement will enable a real speed-reader to take in the chunks on either side at a glance.

Theory 5   While 'mouthing' the words you read may slow you down, sub-vocalisation (saying to yourself) or internal verbalisation is a vital part of learning to read and is necessary for understanding of content.

Technique   Try to push down any sub-vocalisation to a semi-conscious level so that it still aids comprehension, but doesn't interfere with rapid eye movement over the text.

Theory 6   Reading actively and with purpose, i.e. knowing what you want from a text, will enable faster and more efficient reading and comprehension.

Technique   SQ3R or PASS.

Faster reading and 'smarter' reading

You should practise all the techniques learnt above for different types of 'information-gathering' reading (i.e. not novels!). They will work better in conjunction with any helpful **reading strategy** that focuses on prediction, questioning and active reading, while skimming and scanning the material.

Putting it all together

Stage 1

Once you have read the theories explained above and understood the techniques, it is time for you to put them into practice.

The simplest way to do this is to start with a short piece of non-fiction text of average difficulty about a subject that you are interested in (for example, an article in a magazine or a newspaper article).

Use a **reading strategy** to survey how it is laid out and preview its contents. This will help you think about why you are reading a particular text and what information you are trying to extract from it.

When you are sitting comfortably, feeling alert and motivated then try putting the techniques into practice as you read the article.

Don't worry if you can't remember all of them or back-skip the occasional word, or whatever. Rome wasn't built in a day, as they say, and nor will you immediately unlearn years of inefficient reading habits.

But **with regular, sustained practice and motivation your reading speed will improve**.

At first you may feel that you didn't understand much of what you read as you were concentrating so hard on trying to remember the new techniques. But the more you practise and the more automatic the techniques become to you, the more your reading and comprehension will start to improve. **You have to trust** your cognitive abilities to make sense of what they read – the focused brain always tries to make sense of what it is presented with. It's a basic survival mechanism.

Stage 2

When you feel that your actual reading is faster and that you are using the techniques without thinking about them, then start evaluating your comprehension of the texts.

After a short, concentrated reading exercise, stop and:

1. Question yourself about the content.
2. Try paraphrasing what you have read as if you were explaining it to someone else. After all if you can't put it into your own words, you probably haven't understood it very well.
3. Try writing a brief summary of the main points of what you have read including as much detail as possible. Check this with the original text and see what you have missed out.

Note that this procedure can be associated with the SQ3R reading strategy where step 2 above corresponds to the 'recall' stage of the strategy and step 3 above corresponds to the 'review' stage of the strategy, and simply extended by making notes.

Stage 3

Soon you should feel ready to apply your newfound faster reading techniques on actual academic texts. Again, it is best to start off doing this for short, concentrated periods when you are feeling fresh and motivated.

Gradually you can start to extend these reading sessions, from a few paragraphs to a section, from a section to a chapter. **Eventually you will find that you are able to 'click' into this accelerated way of reading for a longer period without fatigue and with concomitant accelerated comprehension**.

Again keep checking your comprehension: what were the main points of what you read, what were the less important points, what were the peripheral details?

CASE STUDY

A 25-year-old exchange student at a university in London had self-referred to the dyslexia department as he found he was struggling with the reading load of his course in Geography. Not surprisingly, an assessment for extra exam time before Christmas revealed that his

(Continued)

overriding weakness was reading speed, at 91 wpm for oral reading and 127 wpm for silent reading. Clearly if his reading speed could be improved, many of the problems he reported, such as poor concentration, an inability to keep up with the work, and patchy comprehension, would be improved too.

Over the next 8 weeks he worked with his tutor on a programme designed to address his slow reading; he was introduced to the theories behind how we read and the techniques needed to be a smart reader, as well as learning SQ3R. For him, this programme meant re-educating reading habits he had practised since boyhood. As he noted in an email following his initial assessment, 'I didn't really get the context straight away because I put so much effort into the reading process.' He was using all his efforts in the mechanical task of reading, so there was little left for memory or cognitive interaction. At week 5 he achieved his highest reading score of 495 wpm with high comprehension, when he was reading about a topic he was really interested in, but this fluctuated over the next 2 sessions to below 400 wpm. What seemed sensible for this student was to aim at achieving and maintaining a comfortable reading speed of around 350–400 wpm together with a 'smart' reading strategy like SQ3R.

If he worked at this, it would not only help him overcome his difficulties at university, but also prove invaluable for his professional life.

Quick summary for learning to read faster and understand more

- Keep your eyes on the page – don't let them stray!
- Be active when you read – question what you want to find out and think about what you know about it already. SQ3R is a simple and effective strategy to help with this.
- Resolve to only move forwards – don't back-skip even if you don't understand a particular word or have missed a word.

(Continued)

(Continued)

- Don't mouth the words but sub-vocalise them to enhance the 'thought stream' of words in your head.
- Use a pencil or chopstick or knitting needle to guide your eyes quickly forward across the page.
- It is better to read fast for short periods – a chapter of a book, a section of an article – than to lose concentration trying to read over a longer period.
- Sit upright in a chair that supports your back with the text on a desk in front of you.
- Practising fast reading regularly will improve your speed and with it your levels of comprehension.
- Motivation is everything. You CAN improve your reading speed and comprehension if you decide to work on it.

POINTS TO REMEMBER

- It is not important for you (or most of us) to aim to read faster and faster. **Your aim should be to achieve and maintain a comfortable, efficient speed that serves your professional and personal needs, with good comprehension**.
- As McLoughlin *et al.* soundly observe, 'Good readers vary their reading rate and comprehension level as a function of materials being read' (2003, p. 63) and also significantly, 'A good reader uses meta-cognitive skills in reading, is aware of the purpose of reading and differentiates between task demands' (2003, p. 63).
- Cottrell (2003, p. 125) makes the same point and provides examples of particular types of text for which slower reading may be more appropriate.
- Finally it is worth observing that, as with any self-help system, how much you achieve will depend on how much you put in. **If you work at trying to read faster, and keep self-evaluating, before long you will see results**. It is about trusting yourself, having confidence that you can improve, and wanting to.

5 Answering Essay Questions

Sandra Hargreaves

This chapter outlines the main stages in planning essays:

- 'unpacking the question';
- brainstorming or mind mapping to put down everything you can think of about the topic;
- writing a theme for your essay to give you direction;
- organising your brain storm or Mind Map™ into a sequential plan;
- writing the essay in workable 'chunks'.

How often have you left your essay writing until the last moment and greatly regretted it? You're not the only one. Read the following case study and see what you can do to change your approach.

CASE STUDY

Sarah was a very disorganised student who always panicked about writing essays and who thought that they were something you couldn't learn to do. She always left them until the last moment and then made a mad rush to the library to collect as much information as she could and often sat up all night writing the essay before handing it in the next day. Essays meant stress and exhaustion. When she discovered that they

(Continued)

(Continued)

could be approached systematically she was surprised but willing to try the approach. After several attempts to write essays in this way she was amazed at the difference in both her own personal well-being and the quality of the essays. She now uses a run-up period of about six weeks to write major essays and goes through the steps: type of question, type of answer, key words, general issues and theme before moving on to the essay plan, the research and the essay itself. She organises the essay into manageable sections ('chunks') for writing. She also finds that she now has time to reread and edit her work after leaving it for a few days. Her marks have improved dramatically and she is no longer upset and stressed at the prospect of writing an essay. She is now so familiar with the technique that she can use it in examinations to prepare essays quickly and thoroughly. She also feels more confident that she has 'answered the question' as she has analysed it so carefully.

Unpacking the question

The first thing you must do is to **make sure that you understand the question**. Many dyslexic students have come to grief in essays and examinations by not reading or interpreting the question properly. Sometimes words are not understood and therefore a different interpretation is given. If you don't know what a word means, **look it up in the dictionary**. If you don't understand specific terminology, **go to your textbooks or ask your subject tutor**.

Analysing the type of question asked

It is essential to spend time on this stage of the essay. Table 5.1 has a list of **commonly used instruction words** with a definition or explanation of what they mean to make things easier for you. I first encountered it when teaching essay-writing skills in Sydney many years ago, but I haven't found anything better and many students find it helpful.

Table 5.1 Commonly used instruction words in essay questions

ACCOUNT FOR		give an **explanation** as to why.
ANALYSE	(1)	**examine** closely, break the subject up into the main ideas of which it ls **composed**.
	(2)	**examine** a subject in terms of its components and show how they interrelate.
COMPARE		discuss the similarities and differences of two or more subjects, theories, etc., **stressing the similarities**.
CONTRAST		discuss two or more subjects, **emphasising their differences**.
DEFINE	(1)	**explain** (make clear) what is meant by.
	(2)	use a **definition** or definitions to explore the concept of, or state the terms of reference of.
DESCRIBE		present an **account** of, show that you understand the topic by writing about it in clear, concise English.
DISCUSS	(1)	investigate a subject, present an account of.
	(2)	consider and offer some **interpretation or evaluation** of.
ENUMERATE		give a **listing** or item by item account of.
EVALUATE		attempt to form a **judgement** about, appraise the clarity, validity or truth of a statement or argument against a set of criteria.
EXAMINE		**inspect** and **report** on in detail.

(Continued)

Table 5.1   (Continued)

EXPLAIN	(1)	make clear the **details** of.
	(2)	show the **reason** for or underlying cause of, or the means by which.
ILLUSTRATE		offer an **example** or examples to:
	(1)	show how or that.
	(2)	show the reason for or underlying cause of, or the means by which.
INDICATE		focus **attention** on.
INTERPRET		set forth the meaning of; **explain** or elucidate.
JUSTIFY		show to be **just** and warranted.
LIST		same as **enumerate** – give an item by item account of.
OUTLINE		go through the **main features** of.
PROVE		show by **logical argument.**
RELATE	(1)	**tell**.
	(2)	bring into or **establish association**, connection or relation.
REVIEW	(1)	**report** the chief facts about.
	(2)	offer a **critique** of.
STATE		declare definitely or **specifically.**
SUMMARISE		describe in **brief** form.

This list is not exhaustive. Can you think of **any other instruction words** and if so, what kinds of demands are made by them?

Often questions are framed without explicit instruction words. They may be in the form of direct questions as follows:

- What is the minimal organisation for living organisms?
- What do you understand by the term 'money supply'?
- Why is Heathcliff such a destructive force in *Wuthering Heights*?
- How did medieval governments obtain the resources to govern?

The approach required by such questions can quite easily be seen by relating them to the implied instruction word. **What is/are** is like **outline** or **describe**, and calls for exposition of the main facts. **What do you understand by** is like **explain,** as are **how do/does/did**. **Why** is like **account for**.

While you are analysing the question you should be thinking of the type of answer the question calls for.

Planning your essay

Types of essays

There are basically five types of essay, which fall into two broad categories – namely, those which are intended to inform and those which are used to persuade. Notice how the types of essay outlined in Figure 5.1 correspond with the question types listed above and noted at the end of each type.

An example of facing the question

Suppose you have been presented with the following question:

Why is Tony Blair such a successful politician?

- First, you should **analyse the question for what it is asking you to do.** It is basically an **evaluative question**, which requires you to give a judgement on Tony Blair's success.
- Secondly, you should **decide what type of essay the question requires**. In forming your judgement as to Tony Blair's success, you need to think about the **criteria** you intend to set up to evaluate him, such as intelligence, integrity, popularity, etc.
- Thirdly, you should **underline the key words** in the question as follows:

Writing to **inform**	EXPOSITORY	**presents** established information in an **orderly manner**, either in classes, or in terms of a scale. OUTLINE, REVIEW (1), STATE, LIST, DESCRIBE
	EXPLANATORY	**accounts for** a phenomenon in the generally accepted way, showing how or why it happens (or happened), in terms of **interaction** within a system, or **cause and effect**. ACCOUNT FOR, ANALYSE (2), EXPLAIN (2)
Writing to **persuade**	INTERPRETIVE	**presents** an individual **interpretation** of a body of data or literature, supported by a consistent set of **features** or **examples** from it. The interpretation is expressed in terms of a key word or phrase, or a classical model. DEFINE (2), DISCUSS (2), INTERPRET, RELATE (2)
	EVALUATIVE	**presents** and justifies a **value judgement**, usually vested in a word of rather relative meaning (e.g. important), which needs to be linked up with certain clearly articulated criteria. The criteria normally imply scales against which individual cases may be ranked. EVALUATE, REVIEW (2)
	ARGUMENTATIVE	aims to **support a given proposition** by means of **logical reasons**, arguing their **validity**, and challenging the validity or relevance of any opposing arguments PROVE, JUSTIFY

Figure 5.1   Definitions of essay types and instruction words which indicate their use

Why is Tony Blair such a **successful politician?**

- Fourthly, you should **think about the major issues**, which hang around the specifics of the question, and the larger context in which your discussion will be set. For example, which politician might you compare Tony Blair with?

Brainstorming or mind mapping

The next stage in essay writing is to put down everything you can think of about the topic. This helps you to find out **what you already know** about the topic and **what you need to research**. A convenient way of doing this, especially if you are a **visual** learner, is to construct a **concept map**. This can be done with pens and paper (large sheets of A3 are the best) or by using a software program such as Inspiration or Mind Manager. Make sure you use lots of **colour**, as this helps you retain the images in your mind.

Consider the essay question: 'What makes **Jane Eyre**, a novel set in the **nineteenth century** and written by the **isolated** and impoverished daughter of a **Yorkshire** vicar, so **relevant** to **modern** life that it is regularly presented in both **dramatic** and **cinematic** form?' Discuss.

After following the steps suggested above you would have decided that the question is asking you to **explain** why you think the novel is still **relevant** and to write an **interpretative** essay in which you would refer to **features** of the novel and **examples** from it. You will have also underlined the key words to direct your attention to them.

The next stage is to **brainstorm** all your ideas into a Mind Map™ by hand or using software. Using Inspiration you may come up with something like Figure 5.2.

Writing a theme for your essay

This gives you **direction**, which will help you to stay on task and not wander off the topic. The theme can be expanded into the introduction and should cover what you are going to say in the essay.

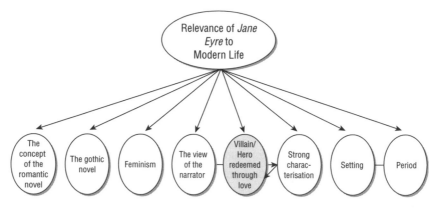

Figure 5.2   Mind Map™ of essay on *Jane Eyre*

Theme: ***Jane Eyre* is so relevant to modern life that it has become a major industry, with recent adaptations for a West End Play, a BBC mini-series and a full-length film.**

Organising your brainstorm or Mind Map™ into a sequential plan

A **concept map can be changed into other formats** very easily, and then put into a **sequential plan or outline**, as illustrated below. The notes, which were made on each theme identified in a balloon in Figure 5.2 have appeared below each subheading in the outline. This was done on the Inspiration program. If this is to be done from a handwritten concept map, you will have to decide on the order that best illustrates your theme.

Plan of the essay based on the concept map of relevance of *Jane Eyre* to modern life

The concept of the romantic novel

The romantic novel is the basis of a huge money-making industry run by publishers who specialise in it. The novel still fits this genre, even though it has many other literary qualities.

(*Continued*)

The gothic novel

The gothic nature of the novel, seen in the intriguing events, which unfold at Thornfield, is timeless.

Feminism

The concept of the defenceless woman with no support and the strength she displays in the novel is very appealing to all ages and periods.

The view of the narrator

The fact that the novel is subtitled 'an Autobiography' is interesting. The novel throughout is narrated from Jane's point of view. Her dilemma is one which all women could relate to and her moral decision is appropriate for the period.

Villain/Hero redeemed through love

This aspect is very appealing to modern readers/viewers and makes the novel timeless.

Strong characterisation

Very strong characterisation evident in many minor characters such as: Mrs Fairfax, Grace Poole, Blanche and Adele, as well as the main characters. This makes the novel alive and interesting.

Setting

Two country estates: the first belonging to Jane's Uncle Reed's family and the second to Mr Rochester. The school where Jane is sent and where her friend Helen dies is another location and based on the school Charlotte Brontë attended. The use of stately homes and schools, which existed in the period, give authenticity and interest to the setting.

Period

Novel written in the nineteenth century and published in 1847. Period usually very well depicted in the modern films and mini-series.

At this stage of your plan **you may decide to reconsider the order** in which you intend to present your argument and you should **change the order if it would be more appropriate**. This is simply done by cutting and pasting.

If the intention was to write the essay in the order of the arguments presented above, you might expand your theme into an introduction something like the one below:

> Theme: ***Jane Eyre* is so relevant to modern life that it has become a major industry, with recent adaptations for a West End Play, a BBC mini-series and a full-length film**. There are many reasons for this. Although *Jane Eyre* was written in the nineteenth century it is still relevant to modern readers and viewers as it has the genre of the 'romantic novel' and combines elements of both the gothic and feminism. The fact that the hero can be seen as a villain redeemed through love has a timeless quality and the fact that the novel is narrated in the form of an 'autobiography' by its young and innocent heroine is still very appealing to modern readers and viewers. The strong characterisation of many of the minor characters also adds interest to the plot. In film versions of the story the use of well-known stately homes and schools, which existed in the nineteenth century, adds authenticity.

This is the time in your essay planning and writing where **you need to research the areas in which you need information**. It is also the point at which you must consider how much time you have available and allocate time to the various areas.

Writing the essay in workable 'chunks'

This allows you to see your progress and know that you are achieving your goals, staying on task and not feeling stressed. An example of this is to **look at the word count and to break it up into paragraphs** as the outline above shows and to allocate the number of words across the essay to fit in with the number of paragraphs. It obviously doesn't have to be precise but it will help you stay on task and not spend too much time on one area to the detriment of others. **Don't forget that all essays need an introduction, which takes about 10% of the word count, and a conclusion, which takes between 10% and 12% of the word count.**

Examples of chunking your essay depending on the word count

Table 5.2 gives some examples of how you might be able to break up essays of different lengths into manageable chunks and distribute the word count across your plan. Some paragraphs will obviously be longer than others, but if you have an overall idea of about how many words you should allocate to each section of your essay you will see that it is not such a formidable task and it will also prevent you from spending too much time on one aspect of the essay at the expense of other sections.

Table 5.2   Word lengths of sections in typical essays

Total length of essay	2,000 words	5,000 words	10,000 words
Introduction	200 words	500 words	1,000 words
Body paragraphs	4 paragraphs of 400 words	8 paragraphs of 500 words	16 paragraphs of 500 words
	or		
	5 paragraphs of 300 words	9 paragraphs of 450 words	17 paragraphs of 450 words
Conclusion	200–250 words	500–600 words	1,000–1,200 words

Some common forms of essay planning include **SWOT (Strengths, Weaknesses, Opportunities and Threats)** Analyses and a template for these has been prepared on the CD-ROM to help you.

 ⊚ **(GO to SWOT Template and Example on CD-ROM)**

Another useful form of essay planning especially in the Social Sciences is related to thinking of issues in respect to major factors such as **PEST (Political, Economic, Social and Technological)** issues. A template for this is also included on the CD-ROM. It is also known as **STEP (Social, Technological, Economic and Political)**.

(⊚) **(GO to PEST Analysis Template and Example on CD-ROM)**

Referencing, plagiarism and the use of sources

Most assignments will require you to draw upon the writings, research and ideas of others. Every time you state a fact or make an assertion in your piece you should support it with a reference to an original source. **Plagiarism is the use of another person's ideas or findings as your own** by simply copying them and reproducing them without due acknowledgement. Plagiarism is dishonest and constitutes cheating. If discovered (and it will be), it is severely dealt with and may result in your exclusion from a course.

Different organisations, universities, colleges, journals and professional groups have their own preferred methods of referencing. Requirements for referencing in assignments vary between institutions and need to be strictly observed. Ask your tutor for the referencing guidelines for your course.

Referencing

There are basically two major methods of referencing:

- Footnote/Endnote system
- Harvard system.

Footnote/Endnote system
This a numeric reference in the footer at the bottom of the page or end of the essay.

An example:

> ... 'Even after practice, people cannot accurately understand rapid discourse above a definite rate. This maximum rate is 300 words per minute – again ten syllables per second'.[1]

(Foot of page or end of section, chapter or essay)

1. D. Orr, H. Friedman and J. Williams, 'Trainability of listening comprehension of speeded discourse', *Journal of Educational Psychology* 56 (1965), pp. 148–56.

Harvard system

This system uses a brief citation in the text in brackets, with a full reference in the bibliography at the end of the document.

> ... 'Even after practice, people cannot accurately understand rapid discourse above a definite rate. This maximum rate is 300 words per minute – again ten syllables per second' (Orr, Friedman and Williams, 1965, pp. 148–56).

Bibliography

The bibliography comes at the end of the whole piece. All books, articles and other sources referred to in the text should be listed on a reference page(s) at the end of the paper. Entries are arranged alphabetically by author surname.

With footnotes or endnotes – simply restate the details already given in the note, but with the authors' surnames first:

> Orr, D., Friedman, H. and Williams, J., 'Trainability of listening comprehension of speeded discourse', *Journal of Educational Psychology* 56 (1965), pp. 148–56.

With Harvard system – give all publication details, as shown in the footnote above, but with authors' surnames first. Often the date of publication is placed immediately after the surnames as with their referencing system.

> Orr, D., Friedman, H. and Williams, J. (1965) 'Trainability of listening comprehension of speeded discourse', *Journal of Educational Psychology* 56, pp. 148–56.

This is a very brief explanation of the two systems of referencing; it is vital to look up your university or college course guide. There is a link to a typical referencing guide on the CD-ROM:

⊚ **(GO to Bournemouth University Citing References on CD-ROM)**

Finishing up

Finally always remember to **reread and edit your work at least 24 hours after you have finished your essay** so that what you are reading is **what you have written** and **not what you think you have written**. Some students find using a text reader, such as TextHELP very useful at the editing stage as some dyslexic students cannot see their errors but they can hear them.

Getting your essay back from your tutor

When you get your essay back from your tutor you should read their comments carefully, and in a positive frame of mind. They are intended to be supportive and the advice they give can be used in the future to help with your next essay. So if you don't understand them, do not hesitate to ask your tutor to explain them.

Some comments will be on the content of the essay, and others will be directed towards structure and language. Insufficient or incorrect content indicates that you may need to do more research and widen your reading. Comments suggesting that you have not answered the questions mean that you need to spend more time analysing the question and planning your work. If you feel that the comments on language and structure are beyond your capabilities to correct, you should seek help from the college learning support or dyslexia support teams.

Planning checklist

The checklist shown in Table 5.3 has been made out for the first essay question discussed in the chapter. This template is available on the CD-ROM.

⊙ (GO to Planning Your Essay – Checklist on CD-ROM)

Table 5.3   Planning your essay – checklist

Unpacking the question	Instruction words: **Why** is				
	Key words: Tony Blair such a **successful politician**?				
Essay type	Expository	Explanatory	Interpretive	Evaluative	Argumentative
				X	
Brainstorm	What you know				
	• Three terms in office • Charismatic • Interviews well • Good use of ministers/spin • Good connections • Good international relations				
	What you need to research				
	• Periods of main ministers in office • Relations with EU • Relations with US • Comparison with Mrs Thatcher				
Theme	**Direction**: Essay is actually asking you to say **why** Tony Blair is a **successful politician**. The question is not asking you to consider the possibility that he is not successful.				
	Tony Blair is a successful politician because he uses the media well, has a charismatic personality, has chosen his ministers carefully and developed good international relations with both the US and the EU. He has been so successful that he has been elected to office for three terms.				
Chunks	Introduction: expanding the theme				
	Body paragraphs: Use of Media Personality Ministers Relations with US Relations with EU Comparison with Mrs Thatcher				
	Conclusion: summing up your points				

(◉) (GO to Planning Your Essay – Checklist on CD-ROM)

POINTS TO REMEMBER

In preparing and planning your essays:

- analyse the question and work out what it is asking you to do;
- work out the type of essay the question requires;
- underline the key words;
- think about the general issues relating to the question and prepare a Mind Map™;
- write a theme for your essay to give it direction;
- organise your concept map into a sequence of points or essay plan;
- reorganise this plan in the light of your research to make sure it flows well;
- write your essay in workable chunks of text so that you can see what you are achieving and don't lose the direction of your argument;
- be prepared to seek or ask for more expert help if this is appropriate;
- check your references;
- reread and edit your work.

6 Structuring Different Writing Genres

Helen Birkmyre

This chapter:

- describes the difficulties that are faced by dyslexic students when attempting to write in different genres;
- outlines a simple formula for paragraph writing – the Point Evidence Comment (PEC) method – and thus helps you to write coherent paragraphs;
- provides a framework for reports;
- outlines the function of abstracts, literature reviews and reflections and how to construct them.

Constructing coherent paragraphs

Essay writing, whether for coursework or examination script, is the predominant method of assessment after the age of 16 but many subjects require different forms of writing. Arguably, college or university students experience more difficulty with formal writing than any other task. This is because it requires so **many different skills** that need to be performed simultaneously, **such as generating ideas, getting them down on paper, sentence construction, spelling and grammar**. Dyslexic students often have trouble expressing their ideas clearly and in a logical, sequential order. A common problem is that they include lots of points in one paragraph without fully explaining them. Dyslexic students also tend to meander, finding it difficult to make points clearly. An effective way to tackle these problems is to create a framework for the information using the **Point Evidence Comment (PEC) paragraph formula**, which can be found in *The Good History Student's Handbook* edited by Gilbert Pleuger (Slattery and Pleuger, 2000). This formula can be used for writing essays as well as the other writing genres: reports and reflective learning journals.

The Collins Online Dictionary defines 'paragraph' as follows:

> [in a piece of writing] one of a series of subsections each usually devoted to one idea and each usually marked by the beginning of a new line, indentation, increased interlinear space, etc.

You can think of your **paragraphs as being mini essays**, with an **introduction (point), main body (evidence) and comment (conclusion)**. Gordon Jarvie, in the *Bloomsbury Grammar Guide* (2000), states that 'a paragraph should be seen as a unit of thought and not a unit of length'. **You should consider only one point per paragraph**. Having one point per paragraph makes it easier for the reader to process the information being provided. You will not be rewarded with a good mark if you do not fully explain the points you are making.

Point

After you have interpreted the question carefully and decided on the points you wish to include using a concept map or similar form of brainstorming (see Chapter 5) you can begin to structure your essay using the PEC formula. **You should first make sure that the point you are making relates directly to the question asked**. Ask yourself, '**Does this point relate to the question?**' If it does, then keep it in your essay. If not, leave it out. Irrelevant points can only weaken your argument. The **first sentence is also known as the topic sentence** because it lets the reader know what the topic of the paragraph is. In the opening paragraph of the introduction this sentence should refer to the question or title.

Evidence

It is vital that you support your point with relevant evidence. **Evidence can be quotations from reliable sources, statistics, examples or visual images.** You can use more than one of these to back up your argument. The stronger the evidence you can provide, the less likely the marker will be to deduct marks. An excellent account of how to use evidence is provided by Bryan Greetham in *How to Write Better Essays* (2001).

Comment

This is your opportunity to demonstrate **your ability to critique and analyse the information you have provided**. In order to demonstrate your point of view it is not sufficient to merely make the point. You have to comment on it as well. **A sentence or two enables you to explain why your point is relevant**. Do not write, '*I think that* … ' Academic conventions dictate that **you do not normally write in the first person** except in reflective journals and similar pieces of work where you will be encouraged to write in the first person. (See the 'Reflective learning journals' section below.) Check with your lecturer, if you are uncertain.

The phrase that you use for your comment will depend on the strength of your evidence, as shown below:

If the evidence is strong:

- It is clear, therefore, that … .
- It is without doubt the case that … .
- It is evident that … .
- Therefore, it is probable that … .
- It is likely that … .

If the evidence is less strong:

- It is possible that … .
- It is unlikely that … .
- It could be argued that … .
- The evidence suggests that … .

CASE STUDY – USING PEC

Kate, a student who had just started her first year of university, required assistance with her essay writing because she was not fulfilling her potential. Her grades for these were low average to below average for her A-level work. Structuring her essays, paragraphing and sequencing points were her greatest weaknesses. Her answers tended to wander aimlessly, lacking structure. She was unsure of how to introduce an essay so they were weak from the very beginning. She had points that belonged in the conclusion in the introduction and there was an overall lack of coherence. Some of her paragraphs were very long and were not written correctly. She had many points in her paragraphs that were undeveloped. Some of her paragraphs were not relevant because she had not made it clear how they related to the question. This can happen when a point is not introduced clearly. Kate often didn't support her points with evidence, using few examples to substantiate her claims. She needed to get into the habit of making a point, supporting it with evidence and then commenting on the evidence in order that her essays had a coherent argument and structure. It was clear that Kate had the ability to make good points as there were many in her work but they were not substantiated or explained fully. She had no idea about the function of a paragraph or how to structure one.

As a result of her difficulties her essays had no clear argument and she failed to answer the questions properly. After working on analysing essay questions and paragraph structure, her first university essay was a remarkable improvement on her previous essays. On her lecturer's marking sheet for the essay she was given 'very good' for 'understanding and discussion of relevant material', and a 'very good' for 'identification of key points and coherent essay structure'. The tutor commented that it was 'well-organised material and focused'. The tutor also said it was one of the best in the year. By using strategies to analyse the question and using the PEC formula for paragraphing, Kate's essay writing went from mediocre to one of the best examples in her year.

Linking paragraphs

Even assuming that you are able to have a clear purpose and a good plan, there are techniques used by good writers to get everything to 'hang together'. Each paragraph will be related to the one before and the one after. This is **coherence**.

There are two main techniques that you can use to help in achieving coherence:

- Try to use words that signal to the reader the connection between ideas. Words like **'therefore'**, **'thus'**, **'hence'**, **'on the other hand'**, **'conversely'**, **'secondly'**, **'for example'** and **'similarly'** tie ideas together or to the main theme of your essay. They direct the reader's attention to the relationships that you are proposing.
- By repeating key words again, the reader's attention is drawn back to the main theme and the relationship of this particular paragraph to it. Key words and key ideas are used too seldom in many essays and while their absence can affect the reader (by making the essay hard to follow), their absence can also affect the writer.

Thus, you may find that because you did not use a key word, that your own attention has wandered off the main theme and that you are including irrelevant material. Thus the repetition of key words is valuable on at least two counts.

Of course the repetition of the same word again and again may irritate the reader. An alternative method is to use another word or phrase with the same meaning. For instance, instead of using the phrase 'key words' in the above paragraph, I could have used such phrases as **'important words'**, **'central ideas'** or **'key themes'**.

You may use a thesaurus to help you find words that may be substituted for others. A word of warning, however – it is unwise to change a simple word for a complex one.

If you practise trying to get coherence in your essays, you will certainly succeed. Your writing may win no prizes for literature, but then no one has won a prize for literature whose writing did not cohere.

Writing reports, abstracts and literature reviews

Before you begin writing assessed pieces of work **ensure that you have read your handbook and/or criteria for the piece of work**. The handbook should specify the elements that need to be included, such as an abstract, literature review, methodology and/or results section. If it does not, ask your tutor to tell you what is required.

Reports

Report writing is required for numerous subjects and it is important that you write it in the conventional report-writing format, unless instructed otherwise. Once again, you should follow the PEC formula for paragraphing within reports, where required. However, it is likely that you will need to include paragraphs that do not follow the PEC formula and that are made up of sentences describing or defining a subject for the reader, for instance as in the METHOD section in Table 6.1.

⊚ (GO to Report Writing Template on CD-ROM)

Deal with the piece of work chunk by chunk. If you find yourself getting 'stuck' on one area, leave it for some time and move on to another section. It is likely that when you come back to the section you were 'stuck' on you will have thought of a new perspective to bring to it.

Abstracts

An abstract is an overview of your piece of work. It is not an introduction. Your introduction is a separate entity. It is best to leave writing the

...uld be made up

focused. You should

n the order in which

ide any information

uld also be written in

in the field you are

bout.

iting report abstracts.

clude in your

the key points from

sults, conclusions

ion of the data, but oretical significance	
plicit aims of roduction)	
on to general theory	
parated out from the ly be included within it. ur what new facts can it of the experiment.	

...pleted the p...
...resentation which...
...ference programm...
...they wish to attend. **The...
...t the paper, presentation o...

...e required for some pieces of wo...
...lecturer will tell you whether or not yo...
...it will be stated in the criteria for the p...

...he Online Writing Lab of Purdue University
edu/ provides excellent instructions for writing
author argues that there are **two types of abst...
descriptive. Both informational and descripti...
an overview of the contents of the report.

- **Informational** abstracts should include informati...
  of your report: purpose, methods, scope, results, ...
  recommendations. They should be up to 10 per ce...

- **Descriptive** abstracts discuss the purpose, met...
  report but **not** the results, conclusions and recor...
  should be around 100 words.

The Online Writing Lab highlights that an abstra...
of one or more paragraphs that are **succinct and...
give the overview of the contents of the report i...
you placed them in your text. **It should not prov...
that is not included in the report itself.** It sho...
such a way that people who are not specialists...
researching can understand what your project is a...

The Online Writing Lab also suggests four steps for w...

- Reread your report to **pick out the key points** to in...
  abstract. Highlight them as you read through it. Pick...
  each of these sections: purpose, methods, scope, re...
  and recommendations.

- Write a first draft of your abstract without looking at your report with the purpose, methods, scope, results, conclusions and recommendations in your mind. Do not lift sentences from your report.
- Revise your first draft to deal with any **structural and sequencing problems such as placing of sentences. Edit out any information that is irrelevant.** Add any information that is relevant or that is missing. Make sure that your sentences are succinct. Correct any errors in grammar or spelling.
- **Proofread your final draft.**

If you follow these steps, you should be able to compose a clear and concise abstract.

(GO to Owl at Purdue on CD-ROM)

Literature reviews

For dissertations, case studies, projects and essays you may be required to write a review of the literature on the topic that is the focus of your research. For those reading History this is called the historiography, which is a discussion of the historical literature written on a subject. **The literature review should follow your introduction and is placed before the main body of the essay.**

Writing a literature review is a useful exercise and will help you to gain a broader knowledge of the subject and help develop your ability to analyse and develop critical thinking.

In your literature review you should:

- **Demonstrate your understanding** of the existing knowledge and theories on that subject.
- **Highlight** any debate or controversial issues that are significant.
- **Critique the literature** highlighting the strengths and weaknesses of it and any theories that have been proposed that are more plausible.
- **Establish your opinion** in relation to the authors' views and comment on them. You must not merely describe what the authors have said. In order

to get a good mark it is necessary for you to provide your own opinion on the matter, for instance agreeing with one point of view or another, or elements of the different arguments.

The University of Toronto's *Writing at the University of Toronto* site has an excellent page on Literature Reviews, providing a list of questions to ask yourself about your literature to ensure that you include all the elements that you need.

www.utoronto.ca/writing

When writing your literature review use the PEC strategy in order that you can make your point, support it with evidence and comment on it.

Reflective learning journals

Some courses will require that you keep a set of reflections on what you have learnt throughout your course and your opinions on it. This type of writing is more informal than academic writing and you have more freedom of expression. Phyllis Creme (2000) calls this type of writing, ' "the personal", in University writing'. There are no strict rules that you need to follow; however, here are some guidelines. You should:

- Write in the **first person** – using 'I'.
- Consider **relevant points** that were mentioned in your class and in your research and **your opinion on them** – establishing a critical position.
- Make points about **significant academic texts** and what they mean to you.
- Discuss what you have **learnt**.
- Discuss what you have felt **inspired by**.
- Highlight what **you do not understand fully** and how you plan to go about finding out **more information** on the topic.
- Discuss your **successes and failures**. If you have been successful, try to evaluate why you were. If you failed to do something well, try to evaluate what went wrong and why, and how you can improve.

Keeping your reflective learning journal and expressing your thoughts in a personal manner should help you to:

- process the information relating to your course;
- increase your understanding of the topic;
- establish a **critical position** on the topics you are studying.

Write in logical paragraphs using the PEC formula for many of the paragraphs. You will still be required to provide evidence to support the points you are making and comment on that evidence for much of your writing, despite it being a more personal style.

POINTS TO REMEMBER

- Use the simple formula for paragraph writing – the Point Evidence Comment (PEC) method.
- Write reports under the headings suggested.
- Make sure that your abstracts cover the contents of your presentation, paper or report and that they are concise and clear.
- Read widely and write clear literature reviews to increase your knowledge and establish your line of argument.
- Write reflective learning journals in the first person and more informal prose to help you understand the subject you are studying.

7 Improving Your Grammar, Spelling and Punctuation

Sandra Hargreaves and John Brennan

This chapter outlines the main things you need to know about:

- grammar
- spelling
- punctuation.

Grammar is a topic which many people find difficult, not just dyslexic students. Some basic grammar is essential for writing. This chapter will only deal with the **most essential things** you need. If you would like to know more about grammar, there is more information provided on the CD-ROM. The most important aspects of grammar are:

- the parts of a sentence
- agreement of verb and subject
- the eight parts of speech
- the use of tense.

Spelling can be a difficulty for dyslexic students. This chapter outlines some of the strategies for learning how to spell.

Punctuation is necessary in order to make completely clear what you are trying to say. Incorrect or absent punctuation leads to misunderstanding.

The **most important punctuation marks** are:

- full stops
- commas
- apostrophes
- semicolons
- colons
- question marks, and
- exclamation marks.

Grammar

This concerns the systematic understanding of the features of a language. It is not the purpose of this chapter to look at grammar in detail, but you do need some rudimentary knowledge to overcome problems such as why your sentences might not make sense or are ambiguous and rambling.

The parts of a sentence

Sentences normally contain a **subject** and a **verb**. When editing your work, check that your sentences are complete. If the sentence you are editing does not contain a subject and verb, rewrite the sentence so that it does. **Subjects** are **nouns** or **pronouns**. **Verbs** are **action words** or the verb '**to be**' and the verb '**to have**'. There must also be agreement **between the subject and the verb** so that **singular subjects** must have **singular verbs** and **plural subjects plural verbs**. If pronouns are involved in the sentence, they also must agree.

For example: **The boy meets** his friend every morning at the station.
(Singular subject, singular verb and singular pronoun)

The boys meet their friends every morning at the station.
(Plural subject, plural verb and plural pronoun)

Sentences can contain many more elements, and are often very complex but they are not sentences if they do not contain the basic elements, which are sometimes called the **sentence kernel**.

The eight parts of speech

All words in a language can be identified as different parts of speech (Table 7.1). Words fall into two broad categories: they can either be **content words**, which have meaning in their own right, such as **nouns**, **verbs**, **adjectives** and **adverbs**, or they can be **structure words**, which rely for their meaning on the context of the sentence in which they are used. **Pronouns**, **prepositions**, **conjunctions** and **exclamations** fall into the category of structure words.

Table 7.1   The eight parts of speech

The eight parts of speech	Content words	1	Nouns
		2	Verbs
		3	Adjectives
		4	Adverbs
	Structure words	5	Pronouns
		6	Prepositions
		7	Conjunctions
		8	Exclamations

Finally, on their own, are the **articles – definite (the) and indefinite (a or an)**.

The content words of English

Nouns
A **noun** is the **name** of **something**. There are four types of noun – namely, **common**, **proper**, **collective** and **abstract**. Table 7.2 defines these and gives examples of each.

Table 7.2   Types of noun

Type	Definition	Example
Common	A **common noun** is a noun referring to a person, place, or thing in a general sense. Usually, you should write it with a capital letter only when it begins a sentence.	All the **gardens** in the **neighbourhood** were invaded by **beetles** this **summer**.
Proper	You always write a **proper noun** with a capital letter, since the noun represents the name of a specific person, place, or thing. The names of days of the week, months, historical documents, institutions, organisations, religions, their holy texts and their adherents are **proper nouns**.	**London Metropolitan University** is near **Holloway Road Tube Station**. **Abraham** appears in the **Talmud** and in the **Koran**.
Collective	A **collective noun** is a noun naming a group of things, animals, or persons. A **collective noun** always takes a singular verb in a sentence.	The **flock** of geese spends most of its time in the pasture.
Abstract	An **abstract noun** is a noun which names anything, which you can *not* perceive through your five physical senses.	He was a man of **principle**. Buying the fire extinguisher was an **afterthought**.

Verbs

Verbs are **action words** plus the verb 'to be' and the verb 'to have'. Whether the events in the sentence are indicated as taking place in the **present** or happened in the **past** is indicated by the **tense** of the verbs used in a sentence. The most important tenses are the **present** and the **past**. Both these tenses consist of three different forms – namely: the simple, the continuous and the perfect. Figure 7.1 shows these different forms.

Note that the simple form of the tense uses only the verb itself. The **continuous** form of the tense uses the verb 'to be' plus the present participle **(always ends in 'ing')** of the verb and the perfect form of the tense uses the verb 'to have' and the past participle **(mostly ends in 'ed')** of the verb.

Present tense

Simple	When she **walks** in the room
Continuous	**I am walking** in the rain
Perfect	We **have walked** before

	Simple	Continuous		Perfect	
I	walk	am		have	
You	walk	are		have	
He She It	walks	is	walking	has	walked
We	walk	are		have	
You	walk	are		have	
They	walk	are		have	

Past tense

Simple	When she **walked** in the room
Continuous	**I was singing** in the rain
Perfect	We **had danced** so long ago

	Simple	Continuous		Perfect	
I	walked	was		had	
You	walked	were		had	
He She It	walked	was	walking	had	walked
We	walked	were		had	
You	walked	were		had	
They	walked	were		had	

Figure 7.1   Verbs and tenses

Adjectives

An **adjective** modifies a noun or a pronoun by describing, identifying, or quantifying words. Adjectives can be used in their original form or changed to their comparative and superlative forms if comparing two or more things. The box below outlines these uses.

	Adjectives can be used before a noun	I like **Chinese** food.
Original	or after certain verbs.	The coal mines are **dark** and **dank**.
	We can often use two or more adjectives together.	The back room was filled with **large, yellow Wellington** boots.

Comparative	When we talk about two things, we can compare them. We can see if they are the same or different. Perhaps they are the same in some ways and different in other ways. We can use comparative adjectives to describe the differences.	America is big. But Russia is **bigger**. I want to have a **more powerful** computer. Is French **more difficult** than English?
Superlative	A superlative adjective expresses the extreme or highest degree of a quality. We use a superlative adjective to describe the extreme quality of one thing in a group of things.	Canada, China and Russia are big countries. But Russia is the **biggest**. Mount Everest is the **highest** mountain in the world.

Adverbs

An **adverb** is a word that tells us more about a verb, or an adjective or another adverb.

Adverb	An **adverb** modifies a **verb**. But adverbs can also modify **adjectives** or even other **adverbs**.	The man *ran* **quickly**. Tara is **really** beautiful. It works **very well**.

Many root words in English exist as the four types of function words by simply adding a prefix or suffix, as the box below shows. Certain endings or suffixes such as '**ness**' or '**th**', indicate that a word is a noun while '**en**' indicates a verb and '**ly**' an adverb.

Noun	Verb	Adjective	Adverb
Sweetness	Sweeten	Sweet	Sweetly
Warmth	Warm	Warm	Warmly
Win	Win	Winning	Winningly
Boldness	Embolden	Bold	Boldly

The structure words of English

The **structure words** of the language **rely** for their meaning **on the context** in which they are used and include: pronouns, prepositions, conjunctions and exclamations.

Pronouns
A **pronoun** can replace a **noun** or another **pronoun**. You use pronouns like **he**, **which**, and **you** to make your sentences less cumbersome and less repetitive. The two most important types of pronouns are **personal** and **relative**.

Personal pronouns
A **personal pronoun** refers to a specific person or thing and changes its form as shown below:

Person	Number	Gender	Subject	Object	Possessive
1st	Single	Both	I	Me	My
	Plural		We	Us	Our
2nd	Both	Both	You	You	Your
3rd	Single	Male	He	Him	His
		Female	She	Her	Her
		Neuter	It	It	Its
	Plural	Both	They	Them	Their

Some examples:

Subjective	**I** was glad to find the bus pass.
	You are surely the strangest child **I** have ever met.
Objective	After reading the pamphlet, Judy threw **it** into the bin.
	Give the list to **me**.
Possessive	**My** life has greatly improved since I changed my job.
	His present is on the kitchen worktop.

Relative pronouns
You can use a **relative pronoun** to link one phrase or clause to another phrase or clause. A clause is a group of words containing at least a subject and verb, but not necessarily a full sentence. The relative pronouns are:

Gender	Subject (before verb)	Object (after verb or preposition)	Possessive
Male Female	Who	Whom	Whose
Neuter		Which/That	

Examples:

Subjective	That is the girl **who** tore her dress.
Objective	You may invite **whom** you like to the party.
Possessive	That is the man **whose** car was stolen.

Prepositions
A **preposition** links nouns, pronouns and phrases to other words in a sentence. A preposition usually indicates relationships of some sort:

* Time **After** lunch
* Place **Between** the sheets
* Logical **Against** all odds.

As you can see a preposition is **always** followed by a noun, but there may be an article or adjective in between.

The most common prepositions are:	The book is **on** the table.
about, above, across, after, against, along, among, around, at, before, behind, below, beneath, beside, between, beyond, but, by, despite, down, during, except, for, from, in, inside, into, like, near, of, off, on, onto, out, outside, over, past, since, through, throughout, till, to, towards, under, underneath, until, up, upon, with, within, without.	The book is **beneath** the table. The book is leaning **against** the table. The book is **beside** the table. She held the book **over** the table. She read the book **during** class.

Conjunctions

You can use a **conjunction to link** words, phrases, and clauses.

Co-ordinating	You use a **co-ordinating conjunction** to join individual words, phrases, and independent clauses. The **co-ordinating conjunctions** are: **and, but, or, nor, for, so, yet.**	Lilacs **and** violets are usually purple. Daniel's uncle claimed that he spent most of his youth dancing on rooftops **but** not swallowing goldfish.
Subordinating	A **subordinating conjunction** introduces a dependent clause and indicates the nature of the relationship between the clauses. The most common **subordinating conjunctions** are: **after, although, as, because, before, how, if, once, since, than, that, though, till, until, when, where, whether, while.**	This movie is particularly interesting to feminist film theorists, **because** the screenplay was written by Mae West. **After** she had learned to drive, Alice felt more independent. **If** the paperwork arrives on time, your cheque will be posted on Tuesday. Gerald had to begin his thesis over again **when** his computer crashed.

(Continued)

(Continued)

Correlative	**Correlative conjunctions** always appear in pairs – you use them to link equivalent sentence elements. The most common correlative conjunctions are: **both, and;** **either, or;** **neither, nor;** **not only, but also;** **whether, or.**	**Both** my grandfather **and** my father worked in the steel plant. Bring **either** a green salad **or** a fish pie. Corinne is trying to decide **whether** to go to medical school **or** to go to law school. The explosion destroyed **not only** the school **but also** the neighbouring pub.

Exclamation or interjection

An **exclamation** or **interjection** is a word added to a sentence to convey emotion. It is not gram-matically related to any other part of the sentence. One usually fol-

Ouch, that hurt! **Hey**! Put that down. **Oh** no, I forgot that the exam was today!

lows them with an exclamation mark. Both are uncommon in formal aca-demic prose, except in direct quotations.

Articles

Articles are the two words we use in English before nouns to make them specific (the) or general (a or an before a vowel).

Articles a, an, the	When talking about one thing in particular, use **the**. When talking about one thing in general, use **a** or **an** before **a** vowel.	Think of the sky at night. In the sky there is one moon and millions of stars. So normally we could say: I saw **the** moon last night. I saw **a** star last night. I saw **an** array of shooting stars last night.

Most words in English fit into the above eight categories. If you want to read more about some other words with more specialised uses, go to the CD-ROM.

Spelling

Even if you have learnt many strategies for coping with your spelling, there will still be words which give you trouble. The aim of this section is to outline **some basic spelling strategies** which are helpful to most dyslexic students. The most important thing to remember is that you **can learn to spell words** which are **important to you**, and you should never become discouraged or give up. Remember that spelling is largely visual and that you can only be sure of the spelling of a word by looking at it.

Spelling strategies

Look, Say, Cover, Write, Check

One very helpful spelling strategy, which is multi-sensory and which has been used over many years, is the **Look-Say-Cover-Write-Check** Method of learning to spell. It involves visual, auditory and kinaesthetic processing. There is a template for this method on the CD-ROM. **(GO to Look-Say-Cover-Write-Check Template on CD-ROM)** You should select **6 – 12 words** to learn **each week**. These words should be the words **that you want to be able to spell correctly**. They will probably be taken from your subject area or from new areas of professional practice. The method relies on a **multi-sensory approach** to the learning task and **regular practice**. On a template write the words you wish to learn in the first column. The remaining columns should be used over the following week to practise the words at least every second day (see Table 7.3).

Firstly	You should **look carefully** at the word you are trying to learn. In this first step, you will be actually using some of the other strategies mentioned below. You need to **look at the structure of the word**, to see if there are any **whole words within**

the word or any **groups of letters** which you can remember as a unit. Another way of looking at the structure is to break the word into syllables.

Secondly You should **say the word aloud** to your self, **sounding out any sections** you wish to specially remember.

Thirdly You should **cover the word and then write it** in the second column. Do not copy the word but cover it and write it. **The aim is to put the words in the long-term memory so that they can be recalled correctly**.

Finally You should check the word against the original word in the first column. If you have made a mistake, cross it out and write it in full above the mistake.

Continue with this pattern until all columns are used. Do **NOT** try to learn any more than **12** words at one time. Some students prefer to learn only **4–6** at one time.

Table 7.3   Words displaying a range of spelling strategies

Original Word	Day 1	Day 2	Day 3	Day 4	Final Check
business					
sep**arate**					
ne**cess**ary					
a**cc**o**mm**odation					
hap**hazard**					
telephone					
doub**tful**					
cir**cle**					
carpenter					
solicitor					
gen**ius**					
ingen**ious**					

The words in Table 7.3 have been chosen to specifically demonstrate some of the strategies you might find useful.

Locating a whole word within a larger word

Many students find that if they can locate **a whole word or two within** a larger word, they can remember the larger word. The first two words in Table 7.3 are good examples of words which can be remembered by this strategy. In the word '**business**' there are two smaller words, '**bus**' and '**i**'. In the word '**separate**' there are also two, '**a**' and '**rat**'. Don't forget to use **bright colours** or **diff**erent coloured **highlight**ing to identify whole words within words.

Using mnemonics to remember spelling

Mnemonics (a Greek word meaning memory trigger, and also difficult to spell) can also be used on the two words analysed above. One way of remembering **business** is the mnemonic: 'I catch the **bus** to **business** every day'. This method combines both the **whole words in the word** with the **memory trick**. A way of remembering **separate** is the mnemonic: 'there is **a rat** in **separate**'. Whatever method you choose, if it works, you have done yourself the favour of learning two commonly misspelt words. Mnemonics can also be used to learn the next two words in the list, which are again difficult and commonly misspelt words. A mnemonic for **necessary** is: 'it is **necessary** to wear **one collar** and two **socks**'. Another for **accommodation** is that: 'good **accommodation** has **two helpings of custard** and **two helpings of meat**'.

Breaking words into sections

'**Hap**hazard' is a good example of a word that is best remembered by breaking it into sections. Otherwise you could be confused by the '**ph**' in the middle of the word, which invariably means that the sound '**f**' is indicated as in 'tele**ph**one'. The operative word to remember here is **hazard** with the prefix '**hap**' meaning chance. If you remember it like this, you will never make a mistake of mispronouncing or misspelling it.

Identifying prefixes, suffixes and root words

Identifying commonly used **prefixes**, **suffixes** and **root words** can greatly assist in remembering their spelling. The word '**telephone**' referred to in the last paragraph is a good example of this. The **prefix** '**tele**' means distance while the root word '**phone**' means sound. By recognising this **common prefix**, the spelling of many other common words, such as '**television**' and '**telegraph**', becomes much easier. The recognition of the root word '**phone**', meaning sound, helps with the spelling of many other common words such '**phonic**' and '**phoneme**'. The **suffix 'ful'** is a good example of how early identification of the fact that it only has one '**l**' as a suffix, but is spelt with two '**ls**' when used **as a word on its own**, helps with the spelling of many words such as **peaceful**, **helpful**, **doubtful** and **bountiful**. An internet shortcut to a list of commonly used prefixes, suffixes and root words is on the CD-ROM.

◉ (GO to Prefixes, Suffixes and Syllables on CD-ROM)

You may like to use these as a base for building some new words and learning their spelling.

Using word families
Many words can be grouped into word families for easy recognition. Once you have identified a word as belonging to a particular family you will always recognise it and remember how to spell it. This is similar to the strategy mentioned previously, in that a **word family** can be identified by a particular prefix, suffix or root word. Once you have recognised that the words '**cycle**' and '**circle**' are derived from the same Greek word, it makes them much easier to remember and spell. Many dyslexic students have problems with words ending in '**er**' or '**or**' such as **builder** and **doctor**. To help you remember these, you might like to put them into two families where most of the '**er**' words refer to **trades** such as '**carpenter**', '**plumber**' and '**carrier**' and most of the '**or**' words to **professions** such as '**doctor**', '**solicitor**' and '**professor**'. This categorisation may well upset a lot of people like '**lecturers**' and '**teachers**', who certainly think they have professional roles, but like all spelling rules there are always exceptions and if grouping words into families helps you learn how to spell them, **that is all that is important**. Word families also help you not to confuse two **different words which sound similar** such as '**genius**' and '**ingenious**'. '**Genius**' comes from the **Latin** for '**creative principle**' and is in the word

family with '**genus**, **genial**, **genital** and **genesis**'. On the other hand '**ingenious**' comes from the **Latin** for '**natural talent**'. There are some lists of word families on the CD-ROM if you wish to investigate this further.

A spelling programme
If you feel that your spelling requires a more intensive programme, you might like to try the Multisensory Spelling Programme for Priority Words (MUSP) which appears on the CD-ROM of *Making Dyslexia Work for You* by Vicki Goodwin and Bonita Thomson (2004).

Punctuation

Instructing the jury Judge Rutter got to the crux of the matter with superb clarity when he said you have to determine where the line has to be drawn between the force expected in a rugby match in which a person taking part is deemed to consent and that to which he is not deemed to consent.

Try reading the passage above. It shows why punctuation is important. Punctuation helps the reader to understand the writer's intended meaning, and, furthermore, allows the writer to be precise in expression.

The use of correct punctuation has been popularised through Lynne Truss's book *Eats, Shoots and Leaves*, which has become a bestseller. The title of the book is explained on the dust jacket. The phrase would be correctly punctuated **without the comma** if it is intended to describe the diet of a panda. As it stands it infers that the panda eats before shooting and then leaving. Another example was reported in a local paper on the problems of women giving up smoking. Sir, '*Women usually find it harder to give up smoking than men.*' The reply followed: '*Who is trying to make women give up men, and will they please stop it?*'

The most misused punctuation mark is the apostrophe. This is because people fail to realise that it only has two purposes, which are to show ownership or contraction.

Table 7.4 (overleaf) outlines the major functions of punctuation marks, with examples.

Table 7.4   The major functions of punctuation marks

FULL STOP	1	To mark the end of a sentence:
		The man crept away without a word.
	2	To mark abbreviations:
		R.S.V.P., ref., cont.
SEMICOLON	1	To separate independent main clauses in the same sentence when these aren't connected by a conjunction:
		The invasion began that night; it didn't last long.
	2	To act as a second grade of punctuation, in addition to the comma, in separating items in a series.
		The audience consisted of ten schoolgirls, each with note-book and pencil; two housewives, with restless children in their arms; and an eager-eyed dog, which wagged its tail through the entire performance.
COLON	1	To indicate that either examples or a restatement of what has just been said will follow:
		The fare must be simple: chicken, fresh salad and wine.
		The fare must be simple: things that take no time to prepare.
	2	To indicate that a quotation of direct speech is to follow.
		NB A comma may also be used for this.
		The stranger raised his voice: Is there anybody there?
COMMA	1	To separate phrases and clauses which might otherwise, in the given arrangement of words, be misconstrued:
		A hundred metres below, the bridge was flooded.
		He was not cheerful, because he fell into the water.
		NB A comma marks off a phrase or clause which is the writer's added comment on the subject:
		The best policeman is the Irishman, who is large enough and vocal enough to inspire respect.
		Contrast the effect of leaving the comma out, which makes the same phrase or clause restrict the subject:
		The best policeman is the Irishman who is large enough and vocal enough to inspire respect.
	2	To set off an interposed phrase or clause:
		His father, the president of the club, appointed him.

		A trainee, however keen he is initially, won't want to continue at that pace.
	3	To separate items in a simple series:
		The audience consisted of ten schoolgirls, two housewives, a policeman and an eager-eyed dog.
APOSTROPHE	1	To mark possession:
		Max's approach, the novel's setting, the cars' horns.
	2	To mark the omission of a letter or letters:
		couldn't, they're, I'm tired.
QUESTION MARK		To mark a question:
		How goes it?
EXCLAMATION MARK	1	To mark an exclamation:
		Heaven help us!
	2	To mark a command:
		Let my people go!
QUOTATION MARKS (Inverted Commas)	1	To enclose actual words spoken:
		He said: 'I'm not coming.'
	2	To enclose a quotation of any kind:
		Few people I've met have such a 'do or die' attitude.
	3	To mark foreign words or phrases, or words or phrases under discussion:
		'carabinieri', 'bête noire', the term 'democracy'.
		NB A common alternative practice is just to underline such words or phrases.
DASH	1	To indicate a break in the grammar of the main sentence:
		He sang loudly – I found him far too loud – and with little sensitivity.
	2	NB Brackets are an alternative way of marking off an interjected, explanatory or qualifying remark.
		He sang loudly (I found him far too loud) and with little sensitivity.
		To show that what follows is a summary addition to the sentence:
		The applicant shows energy and initiative – both essential to the task.

There are exercises on punctuation in the CD Rom if you would like to see if you can put your new punctuation skills into practice.

(GO to Punctuation Exercises on CD-ROM)

There are several quick links to other information on grammar, spelling and punctuation on the CD-ROM.

POINTS TO REMEMBER

- Make sure that all your sentences contain a subject and a verb (sentence kernel).
- Keep your sentences short. A sentence that runs on over two lines is usually too long.
- You CAN learn to spell words which you want to learn to spell by using a variety of strategies.
- Make sure that your sentences make sense and say what you intend them to say by using correct punctuation.

---

8 Improving Mathematics Skills and Using Statistics

Judith Cattermole

This chapter:

- outlines strategies using concrete materials to help you overcome maths problems;
- outlines the two main approaches to tackling maths problems;
- demystifies the symbolic language of maths;
- suggests ways of learning formulae, if necessary;
- suggests strategies for overcoming problems with fractions and decimals;
- suggests strategies for overcoming problems with statistics.

If you have sometimes experienced problems with arithmetic or working with numbers, then you may find this chapter helpful; especially if your coursework requires an ability to work with **fractions, mathematical formulae, decimals and statistics**. In this chapter you will find some strategies that have worked with other students who have had similar problems. It will concentrate on using **concrete materials and exercises**, which have been helpful for students in overcoming their problems.

It is not unusual for dyslexic students to experience difficulties with the mathematical content of their course but just as there are ways of helping you with other study skills, there are strategies you can use to help you solve maths problems. According to Vicki Goodwin and Bonita Thomson (2004), about 60 per cent of dyslexic people have some difficulties with maths but these are often to do with *procedures and remembering the order in which the operations should be undertaken* rather than the mathematical concepts.

Thinking (cognitive) and learning styles

In maths it has been customary to refer to the two main cognitive approaches to problem solving as the **inchworm** and the **grasshopper approaches** (Chinn and Ashcroft, 1998). These are simply alternate ways of describing a more **holistic** (grasshopper) approach or a more **analytical** (inchworm) approach. You may have used the questionnaire in Chapter 2 to help you to think about your own cognitive and learning style. The three learning styles – namely, **visual**, **auditory** and **kinaesthetic** – can also be applied to learning mathematical concepts and many of the concrete methods suggested here are a combination of both visual and kinaesthetic styles. You should use the information you gained in Chapter 2 to adapt the advice and tips in this chapter to suit your own cognitive and learning style. In addition to this and in the same way that you may have a preferred approach for dealing with words and letters you may have a preferred approach for solving mathematical problems. The two main types are described below.

Inchworms typically:

- focus on the details;
- work methodically;
- check answers by going through their working from the beginning;
- follow instructions.

Grasshoppers, on the other hand:

- take an overview of the whole problem;
- will probably give an intuitive answer;
- work back from their answer to check if it is correct;
- adjust numbers to make the calculation easier.

You may not clearly fall into one category and feel that **you use different methods to solve different problems**. **Choosing a method of working to suit the task** can be helpful and many people work in this way. If you are having difficulties with a mathematical problem and if you feel that you are working like an inchworm or a grasshopper, it might be helpful to try using different techniques and approaches. Neither method is right or wrong but one can be more helpful than the other for solving different problems.

Useful tips

Wherever possible use **concrete materials** to help you understand processes and concepts. Typical things that students use are: paper, string, coins, buttons and even sweets and chocolate bars. Doing things physically can help you to understand concepts and theories. We shall go into this in more detail in the section on fractions.

Use squared paper for calculations: this will help you to:

- line up numbers, symbols and decimal points vertically and horizontally;
- draw charts, tables and diagrams neatly;
- calculate areas.

Use a **calculator** wherever possible but always try to estimate your answer first, so you know if you have approximately the right answer on your calculator. Choose a calculator with a large display and keys which are easy to press. Do the calculation twice to check if you have the right answer.

Language of maths

Understand the **language of maths**. One symbol can be used to express different everyday words, as demonstrated in Table 8.1.

Table 8.1 The language of maths: common and advanced symbols

Common symbols	
Symbol	**Words**
=	equals, is the same as, equivalent to
+	add, sum, and, plus, total
−	minus, subtract, take away
×	times, multiply, of
÷	divide, goes into, split, share
<	is less than
>	is more than, is greater than
Advanced symbols	
Symbol	**Words**
n^x	means the number n is 'raised to the power $\times$'. So 6^2 means 6×6 (= 36) and 2^3 means $2 \times 2 \times 2$ (= 8). The power of 2 is called 'squared' (6^2 is 6 squared) and the power of 3 is called 'cubed' (2^3 is 2 cubed).
$\sqrt{}$	means 'square root'. This is the number which squared equals the number after the sign. So $\sqrt{n}$ is the number m for which $m \times m = n$. For example $\sqrt{25}$ is 5 because $5 \times 5 = 25$.
Σ	sum of all the numbers
σ	measures the distribution or spread of the data

Formulae are ways of expressing mathematical relationships or rules. They use symbols and letters instead of words, for example:

$$E = mc^2$$

Energy is equal to mass times speed of light squared

E   =   m   (×)   c ^{2}

Notice that in formulae using symbols, the times (x) sign is not included.

Not all colleges and universities require students to remember formulae and will give them to you as part of the exam questions. Others will allow students with dyslexia to take designated help sheets into exams. Find out what your college or university allows you to do rather than using valuable study time in trying to remember something that you don't need to.

Example formulae – converting Centigrade to Fahrenheit

The relationship between temperatures measured in degrees Centigrade (Tc) and degrees Fahrenheit (Tf) is given by the formula:

$$9Tc = 5(Tf - 32)$$

9 times **Centigrade is equal to** 5 times
Opening Brackets Fahrenheit less 32 **Closing Brackets**

9	x	**Tc**		=	5	x
(		**Tf**		–	32	)

This formula has something new – namely, brackets. Brackets are used in mathematics to indicate the order in which operations (adding, subtracting, multiplying, etc.) are performed. If there are multiple operations in a calculation, the order in which they are done will often affect the result. Please see the CD-ROM for this example in coloured type. ☺

In order to be clear rules and procedures have been agreed to define the order of operations in formulae. It is essential to do the operations in the correct order to get the right answer:

- Do things in Brackets first.
  - ✓ $7 \times (4 + 3) = 7 \times 7 = $ **49**   ☺
  - ✗ $7 \times (4 + 3) = 28 + 3 = $ \31   (wrong ☹)
- Powers and Roots before Multiply, Divide, Add or Subtract.
  - ✓ $5 \times 2^2 = 5 \times 4 = $ **20**   ☺
  - ✗ $5 \times 2^2 = 10^2 = 100$ (wrong ☹)

- Multiply or Divide before you Add or Subtract.

  - ✓ $3 + 4 \times 5 = 3 + 20 = 23$ ☺
  - ✗ $3 + 4 \times 5 = 7 \times 5 = 35$ (wrong ☹)

Otherwise just go left to right.

  - ✓ $30 \div 5 \times 3 = 6 \times 3 = 18$ ☺
  - ✗ $30 \div 5 \times 3 = 30 \div 15 = 2$ (wrong ☹)

These rules can be remembered through the acronym BODMAS (see Figure 8.1).

Figure 8.1 BODMAS diagram

B	Brackets first
O	Order (i.e. Powers and Square Roots, etc.)
DM	Division and Multiplication (left-to-right)
AS	Addition and Subtraction (left-to-right)

If you need to remember formulae:

- Write them in a **notebook** in a way that is helpful to you. For example, by using **colour** or **different thickness** of pens.
- write the formula out in words, for example:

Volume	equals	**length**	times	**breadth**	times	**height**
V	=	l	(x)	b	(x)	h

- Use **mnemonics** containing words that are significant to you or something you find amusing. Anything will do as long so you find it easy to remember.

> Anne is a single mother of two toddlers and remembered the Energy formula of the start of this section as:
>
> | Exhaustion | is the same as | mother | times | children | (2) |
> |---|---|---|---|---|---|
> | E | = | m | (x) | c | 2 |

- **Seek help**: If you are receiving tutorial support, make sure that your tutor knows that you have problems with numbers. Some universities and colleges offer specialist numeracy help either to groups of students or individuals. Find out if you are entitled to this type of help.
- **Search the internet**. There are websites which offer help to adults with dyslexia and numeracy difficulties; two of the best are:

  www.bbc.co.uk/skillswise/
  www.dfes.gov.uk/curriculum_numeracy

The Dyscalculia and Dyslexia Interest Group based at Loughborough University provides an opportunity for exchange of information for students and tutors about issues of studying maths in higher education for students from a variety of backgrounds including dyslexic students.

Understanding fractions

Many students find understanding fractions difficult so here are some techniques which you might find helpful. If they don't work for you, then use your imagination to adapt them to suit your own needs and learning style.

(•) **(Go to Understanding Fractions – Folding on the CD-ROM)**

Try this technique of folding paper. It might be easier if you use squared paper which will give you some lines to use for folding.

After you have folded the paper once along the middle you will have two equal parts (two halves), which make one whole. The words **one half** are written numerically as a fraction:

$$\frac{1}{2}$$

You can write this fraction on each piece of paper:

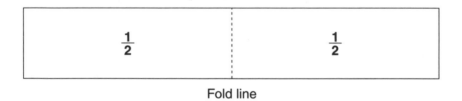

Fold line

Notice that:

- the number under the line tells you how many pieces make a whole one: **the denominator**;
- the number on top of the line tells you how many pieces in that fraction: **the numerator**.

(It is easy to remember: **d**enominator and **d**own start with same letter.)

Fold the paper along the original fold line and then fold it in half again. Open it out. You will now have four pieces (four quarters). The words **one quarter** are written numerically as a fraction:

$$\frac{1}{4}$$

You can write this fraction on each piece of paper:

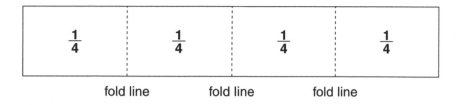

You can carry on folding the same piece of paper for more fractions, which will give you:

Eight pieces:

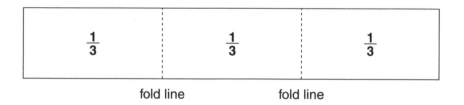

Take another piece of squared paper and this time fold it into three equal pieces to give you thirds:

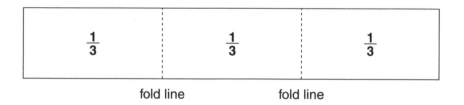

Write the correct fraction in each piece.

If you folded the paper again across the middle, how many pieces would there be?

Alternative approaches

Using colour
Some students find folding the paper fiddly and prefer a different approach using different colours to represent different fractions.

You can try using one piece of grey paper to represent the whole one on which you can lay differently coloured segments of paper to represent halves, quarters, eighths, thirds, sixths, fifths and tenths.

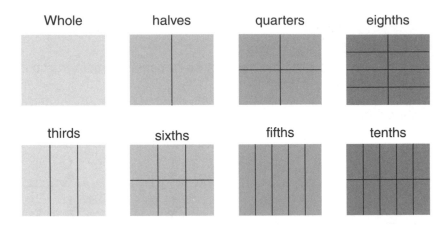

You can **colour code** the different segments to demonstrate the different 'fraction families' and to help you remember the relationship between:

- **halves, quarters and eighths (orange);**
- **thirds and sixths (yellow);**
- fifths and tenths (green).

⊙ (GO to Understanding Fractions – Colour on CD-ROM)

You'll find the Contrasting Colours in the whole-text versions of the book on the CD-ROM.

Using a fraction wall
An alternative approach is to use fraction walls, which are on the CD-ROM. These combine elements of the folding and colour techniques.

⊙ (GO to Fraction Walls on CD-ROM)

Not all these methods will be suitable for everyone; choose the one that works best for you or even better use your own ideas to adapt these methods or make up your own.

On the CD-ROM you will also find some help sheets that explain how to make calculations using fractions. These are intended to be used only as a reminder and backup learning aids and not as a replacement for tactile, visual and verbal techniques you may want to try out for yourself.

Decimals

Like fractions decimals are used to represent parts of things. A decimal number uses a decimal point (a dot) to separate whole things (integers) on the left from parts of things (fractions) on the right.

Examples	$\frac{1}{2}$ = 0.5	$\frac{1}{3}$ = 0.3333	A decimal can be seen as a fraction of tenths, hundreds, thousands and so on.
	$\frac{1}{4}$ = 0.25		
	$\frac{1}{8}$ = 0.125	$\frac{2}{3}$ = 0.6667	So 0.25 is $\frac{25}{100}$
	$\frac{5}{8}$ = 0.625		

Thus if you see a decimal such as 0.216 this means there are:

Two tenths + one hundredth + 6 thousandths

or

$$\frac{2}{10} \quad + \quad \frac{1}{100} \quad + \quad \frac{6}{1000}$$

| hundreds | tens | units | | tenths | hundredths | thousandths |

larger 153.216 smaller

Remember that the whole numbers on the left of the decimal point get larger as they more away from the decimal point but the numbers on the right get smaller.

Test yourself

Put the following decimal numbers in sequence starting with the smallest number first and ending with the largest:

100.6   99.16   9.3   100.59   100.635   9.08   31.5   31.49

Fill in the missing numbers in each sequence

3.97   3.98   3.99   _____

24.97 24.98 24.99 _____   25.01 25.02 25.03

(GO to Understanding Decimals on CD-ROM)

On the CD-ROM there are some help sheets which explain in more detail how to do decimal calculations.

CASE STUDY FOR FRACTIONS AND DECIMALS

Paul was a foundation year Business Studies student who described himself as a failure because he was struggling with the mathematical content of his course. He was particularly concerned about his inability to understand the concept of fractions and decimals. He felt that this was probably due to his dyslexia and his inability to concentrate for extended periods of time. He also said that figures (numbers) often became blurry and he lost his place when looking at a series of numbers. Because of his past failures in maths he said that he felt like giving up before he started with some coursework questions that included fractions and decimals because he found them so difficult to understand.

Paul said, 'I like to visualise things in my head so I can see the whole picture of the problem.' When he was presented with a problem he would give an estimated trial answer and then work backwards to see if he was right. He did not like to write things down but worked things out mentally in his head. Paul said that he liked the challenge that this presented and that writing things out was boring and that seeing the numbers and symbols on the page muddled him up. He did like to work with concrete materials but found the folding of paper method 'fiddly

(Continued)

and time consuming' but he did enjoy working with different coloured paper as this was 'more exciting and visual'.

He also liked the opportunity to add and take away different pieces of paper and immediately saw that if he took away, for example, one quarter from three quarters which were laid over the grey whole one, he was left with two quarters which was equal to half of the whole one. He liked approaching this as a puzzle and working out which pieces he could use.

Statistics

In the following section you can see how a subject like statistics, which many dyslexic students find very difficult, can become more accessible with the use of colour, visual representations and concrete examples. The basic statistical concepts of **mean**, **median**, **mode** and **distribution** are demonstrated through these methods.

Mean, median and mode

A student measured the heights of 11 university students.

The results were arranged in increasing order (rank order), as shown in Figure 8.2.

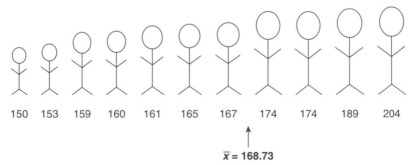

| 150 | 153 | 159 | 160 | 161 | 165 | 167 | 174 | 174 | 189 | 204 |

$\bar{x} = 168.73$

Figure 8.2   Heights of student in rank order

There are three different ways of thinking about an average of a set of numbers:

- Mean (arithmetic average) written as $\bar{x}$
- Median (middle number)
- Mode (most frequent number).

Mean

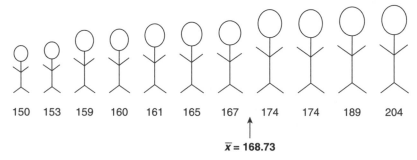

| 150 | 153 | 159 | 160 | 161 | 165 | 167 | 174 | 174 | 189 | 204 |

$$\bar{x} = 168.73$$

Figure 8.3   Student heights – mean

The mean, or arithmetic mean (shown in Figure 8.3), is written as

$$\boxed{\bar{x} = \Sigma \chi / n}$$

Where:

Σ (sigma) the sum of the sample (all the values added together)

n the number of samples (in this example n = 11 people)

χ the value of the sample (the number)

$\Sigma\chi/n$ $\dfrac{150+153+159+160+161+165+167+174+174+189+204}{11}$

$\bar{x}$ **168.73**

Taking another set of numbers – 40, 41, 55, 55, 60, 65:

The mean ($\bar{x}$) is $= \bar{x} = \Sigma\chi/n = $ **40 + 41 + 55 + 55 + 60 + 65**
$$\overline{}$$
$$6$$

$$= \textbf{52.67}$$

In this case, because of the two small readings, the mean is smaller than most of the numbers in the sample.

Median

The median of a group is the middle number in a list when arranged in rank order (Figure 8.4). In the student heights sample, the median is the 6th number:

165

This works for odd numbers, but if the sample is even, then the median is taken as the arithmetic mean of the middle two numbers.

For example, given the set 1, 1, 2, 3, 4, 5, 6, 7:

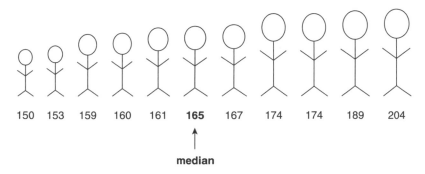

| 150 | 153 | 159 | 160 | 161 | **165** | 167 | 174 | 174 | 189 | 204 |

↑

median

Figure 8.4   Student heights – median

- The median is $\dfrac{\textbf{3 + 4}}{\textbf{2}}$

  $= \textbf{3.5}$

- By contrast the mean $\bar{x} = \textbf{3.63}$

MODE

The mode is the measurement that occurs the greatest number of times. In the case of the student heights, the mode is 174.

Sometimes there may be several modal values in a set of data.

In the set 46, 48, 50, 50, 51, 51, 51, 52, 53, 53, 53:

- There are two modal values: 51 and 53
- The median of this set is 51
- While the mean $\bar{x} = \Sigma\chi/n =$ $\dfrac{46 + 48 + 50 + 50 + 51 + 51 + 51 + 52 + 53 + 53 + 53}{11}$

$$= 50.73$$

Problems

Rank the following numbers then calculate the mean, median and mode.

1   **23, 45, 54, 45, 67, 45, 56, 67, 34**
2   **34, 45, 45, 23, 34, 45, 45, 67, 65, 43**
3   **2, 4, 5, 7, 2, 4, 3, 7, 5**
4   **1, 4, 6, 4, 8, 7, 6, 5, 4, 5**

The answers can be found on the CD-ROM.

(GO to Answers to 3M Questions on CD-Rom)

Normal distribution

Figure 8.5 shows the height (cm) of students in a lecture theatre. The normal curve is a distribution of scores which is symmetrical about the mean – that is, each side is a mirror image of the other. The median, mode and mean will coincide at the centre of the curve – the high point. The further away any particular value is from the mean, above or below, the less frequent that value will be.

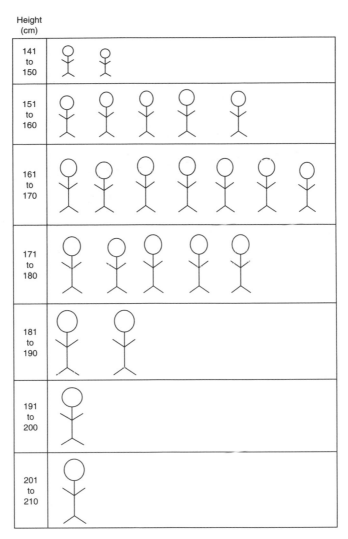

Figure 8.5   Normal distribution

Frequency curve

The frequency curve shows the range of data. This set of results in Figure 8.6 show that the distribution is not symmetrical and the data is

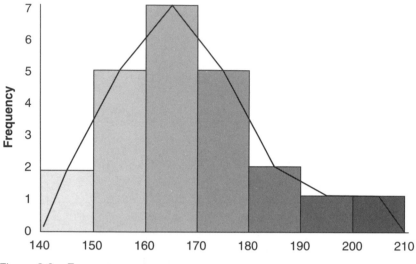

Figure 8.6   Frequency curve

positively skewed (skewed to the left), as illustraterd in Figure 8.7. This indicates that the lower values have a higher frequency, and that there are very few tall people.

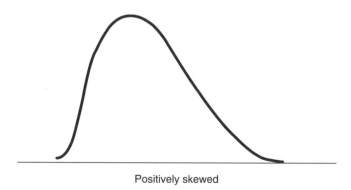

Positively skewed

Figure 8.7   Frequency curve – positively skewed

If the frequency curve is negatively skewed (skewed to the right) as shown in Figure 8.8, then there would be more tall people and few short people.

Negatively Skewed

Figure 8.8   Frequency curve – negatively skewed

If the frequency curve is symmetrical as shown in Figure 8.9, then there is a normal distribution of heights with equal amounts of tall and short people.

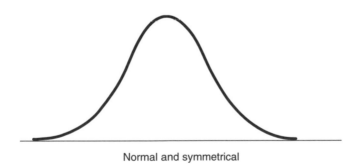

Normal and symmetrical

Figure 8.9   Frequency curve – normal and symmetrical

The range

The range is the difference between the highest number and the lowest number. In the case of the students' heights preserved in Figure 8.2 the range is:

204 − 150 = 54

The mean and the range could be the same, yet the distribution of the data could be completely different.

The standard deviation

The standard deviation is often used to measure the distribution or spread of the data. For a reasonably symmetrical and bell shaped set of data like the one above, **one standard deviation** each side of the mean will include roughly **68%** of the data and **two standard deviations** each side will include roughly **95%** of the data. Therefore the size of the standard deviation is a measure of the spread of the data. If somebody says that the data has a **small standard deviation**, it means that a lot of the **data is grouped closely around the mean**, i.e. there are lots of people of about the same height. If it has a large standard deviation, then there is obviously a wide range of heights in the group.

POINTS TO REMEMBER

Improving mathematics skills

- Use concrete materials as a starting point to help you to understand number concepts and processes.
- Try to use your own learning styles to develop techniques that will help you.
- Be prepared to progress at a rate which suits you.
- Use materials that appeal to your own needs and be prepared to adapt them if necessary.
- Don't be surprised if your progress and development is not regular and be prepared for revision periods.
- Try out different methods and techniques, especially if you seem to be working at either end of the grasshopper–inchworm continuum.
- Be prepared to seek or ask for more expert help if this is appropriate.

(Continued)

Using statistics

There are three possible ways of obtaining the averages from data after you have put it into rank order (rank order increasing value, e.g. 1, 2, 3, ... 7, 8, 9, 10 ...).

- Mean is the average value.
- Median is the middle number.
- Mode is the number which comes up the most times, and can be more than one number.

The size of the standard deviation gives you an idea of the spread of the sample.

9 Examination Techniques

Sandra Hargreaves

When preparing for examinations:

- adopt the right mindset;
- make all the appropriate preparations for your examinations well in advance;
- plan your revision and your exam timetables;
- revise for your examinations according to your cognitive and learning style;
- practise sample examination questions under timed conditions.

This chapter also looks at the **day** before the exam and gives you tips on sitting examinations. There is also some useful advice on how to cope during the examination period.

Having a learning plan and revision timetable and knowing that you are sticking to them will increase your confidence and reduce stress.

Adopting the right mindset

Many dyslexic students would prefer to choose courses that do not contain examinations, as they require recall and written expression under time pressure. These activities can cause dyslexic students big problems as they require good working memory and written expression. You may also wish to discuss alternative methods of assessment (such as giving a presentation) with your tutor or the dyslexia co-ordinator at your college.

If, however, you have to do exams, it is not all doom and gloom. Reasons to love exams include:

- Compared to coursework you need less in-depth research and reading.
- You don't have to write out full references.
- You are allowed more leeway with minor grammatical errors, spellings and forgotten details – though handwriting must stay legible!
- This is your chance to prove what you have learnt.
- You will feel great when you have done them to the best of your ability.
- They are over and done with quickly.

You need to prepare yourself well in advance. Leaving revision until the last moment and '*cramming*' only increases your anxiety. Anxiety causes lack of sleep and poor recall of what you have managed to put into your long-term memory. **The key for dyslexic students is to ensure that all the material you need for examinations is in your long-term memory** where you can draw on it to answer the questions you will be given. With the additional time you are given, as a dyslexic student, for reading and processing the questions and recalling the information you have learned, there should be nothing to make you anxious.

Making administrative preparations

Most colleges have strict cut off dates for notifying the assessment unit of the special provisions to which you are entitled. Every institution will have slightly different arrangements, and it is your responsibility to ensure that the arrangements are in place for you well before every examination period. **You must not assume that just because you have notified the university or college of your dyslexia that the arrangements will be made**. All students have specific arrangements designed to help them overcome their particular weaknesses. All dyslexic students are given extra time so long as they have proven their dyslexia to the institution. The amount of time, however, may vary between students. Some students prefer to use word processors, and some amanuenses (scribes). Others will require readers, or examination papers in different colours or printed in larger font. **Whatever your needs, they should appear in your Needs Assessment and must be agreed with the dyslexia co-ordinator in the institution you attend**. If your institution provides stickers or memos for you to put on your papers to alert the markers to your dyslexia, don't forget to take them with you to the exam.

Many colleges and universities also expect students to notify the assessment unit about the modules they are taking in each exam period so that the examination arrangements, which have to be made with the dyslexia co-ordinator, can be put into place. **Check what your institution expects**.

Planning your revision and your exam timetables

Once all of the administrative arrangements are planned you can begin on the real business of examination revision. **The first step is to write a list of what you need to revise**.

⊙ (GO to Revision List on CD-ROM)

The list of assignments which you prepared at the beginning of the term outlined in Chapter 1 can be modified for this purpose. A blank template is available on the CD-ROM. **Once you know the extent of your revision, you can draw up a revision timetable and an examination timetable**, which again can be based on the timetables described in Chapter 1. Blank templates are also available on the CD-ROM.

⊙ (GO to Revision Timetable on CD-ROM)

Revision timetable

Make sure when you compile your revision timetable that it reflects the requirements of the examination timetable. Be careful that you do not fall into obvious traps such as spending all your time on revising for the first examination and fail to leave time for subsequent examinations.

With your revision timetable, put down realistic time slots for revision and vary your topics across each day. A lot has been written on the subject of attention span but remember that **30–40 minutes of uninterrupted attention** on revision is about as much as the mind can absorb. You should then have a break. Either at the end of the revision session or before starting another session, **recall what you have learnt in the previous session.**

(o) **(GO to Exam Timetable on CD-ROM)**

Exam timetable

Double check, when compiling your examination timetable, that you:

- **Note the correct date for each examination.**
- **Check the time of each examination.**
- **Know where you are to sit each exam.** Many students have destroyed all their preparation in a few moments by going to the wrong examination room, or even the wrong building. Colleges are large and sometimes rambling institutions. During examination periods every available room is often in use, and students frequently have to sit examinations in rooms where they have never been before. **It is imperative to go and find the room in which you will be doing the examination well before** you have to sit for the paper.

Check with your friends to see that they have the same information. Being in the wrong place or at the wrong time is a costly error, as you will then have to resit the examination.

The final preparations, and those which should ensure that you will be successful, are **knowing the location of the room** and going in to take the examination **well rested, well fed, calm and confident**.

Be good to yourself

It is important that you allocate time for relaxation, exercise and plenty of sleep in both the revision timetable and the examination timetable itself.

- Drink plenty of water for optimum brain vitality.
- Eat healthily and at regular intervals. Keep a regular, relaxed routine. Consume caffeine and cigarettes in moderation (if you have to!).
- Build in exercise and movement; it may help you sleep well at night.
- Perhaps revise with like-minded friends. Avoid the ones that make you nervous or undermine your confidence.
- Fix a relaxation technique that you use every day when you are working well. There are a variety of relaxation techniques which can be used, including yoga, meditation and Brain Gym® (Paul Dennison – see 'Further reading').
- Work on staying positive.
- Reward yourself for sticking to your revision schedule, so that you are in peak performance for the big day.

Revising according to your thinking and learning style

Remember, when you begin to revise look at course module outlines, reread key texts and lecture notes and make good notes (see Chapter 3). You should start as soon as possible, keeping to your revision timetable.

Much of what was covered in Chapter 2 applies to examination revision. You might like to go back and review that chapter before proceeding with your revision. Look at the Inspiration concept maps (Figures 2.2, 2.4 and 2.5) to see which revision techniques you wish to use. If you have a **holistic cognitive style, you may wish to prepare an overview of a whole topic** before revising sections of it. This can be done using a concept map or spider diagram. If you are more **analytical, you may wish to learn individual sections and build towards the 'big picture'** of the topic you are covering.

Visual revision techniques

- Create **posters** to display around the room using **bright colours** and **large font** to make the layout clear and eye-catching (see Stefan's case study below).
- **Concept maps** are particularly useful for exam revision. Create new maps for each topic you are revising.
- Use **rooms** in your house for different subjects or topics. When you are trying to recall the information elsewhere, visualise yourself in the room to trigger your memory.
- Use **visual memory pegs** to learn lists of items, dates or terminology. Link the visual peg for the number with the item you are learning.
- Use **index cards** either with points for each topic written in bullets or with a question on one side and points for the answer on the other. It is a good idea to **colour code** your index cards so that you have different coloured cards for each subject or topic.

Auditory revision techniques

- Use **mnemonics** to recall information, such as factual terms and material or even how to spell a word.
- Create **acronyms** to synthesise a set of data, a list of terms or a set of topics into one word (doesn't need to be a real word) so that when you recall it in the examination you can remember all the information attached to it (see Doris's case study below).
- Use **auditory memory pegs** to learn lists of items, dates or terminology.
- **Read your revision cards aloud** or ask a friend or family member to ask you questions so that you can **explain the information you are trying to understand** to them.
- **Record the points** you are revising on a mini-disk or other digital recording device. Play them back when you are doing something else like housework or travelling on the train.
- **Discuss your work** with a friend. You could get together with a classmate and compare your understanding of certain concepts or topics, which of course will help them too.

Kinaesthetic revision techniques

- **Compile study notes** on a mini-disk and **listen to them while walking, cycling or jogging**.
- Write out your notes a few times, **condensing them down to just a few key words** that will trigger your memory of the subject.
- Use **highlighter pens to colour code** different topics or **draw pictures** to relate to the different topics.
- If your assessment includes a presentation, **practise your presentation** in front of someone you know, in the mirror or on video.
- If your assessment includes a practical component, use **role play** as an effective way of putting your knowledge into practice, before the practical examination.

Look at the following case studies. The first is a comment by **a multi-sensory learner**, Stefan, who uses **visual techniques** in the production of **posters** and **index cards**, combined with the **auditory techniques** of **rehearsing the contents of the cards** aloud in front of the mirror or to family members. **Kinaesthetic methods** are also used in **rewriting and condensing notes**.

> ### STEFAN'S CASE STUDY – USING MULTI-SENSORY TECHNIQUES
>
> When I revise, I find a combination of two approaches is the most effective. In the longer-term lead up to an exam (3 or so weeks), I try to write all those important details which are hard to remember (such as lists, quotes, timelines and diagrams) onto posters. I usually just use A4 plain paper, and I make them in lots of eye-catching colours on the computer. With one wall of my bedroom dedicated to each subject (at A2, this means that you get one free wall!), it is a really non-stressed way to revise, since every time I am in my room I'm just able to 'soak it up' without much effort on my part. I can revise by staring at my wall.
>
> The other way I revise is to make notes on index cards. Each subject has its own colour of card (blue for History, yellow for Music, pink for Religious

(Continued)

Studies) and I try to use a few different colours of biro for points, quotes and headings. When I've written a set of notes, I write them all out again but this time trying to condense them. Going through this seemingly endless 'condensation' process is what gets it drilled into my mind. The other bonus is that I can always carry them around in my pocket and have a look at them whenever I'm waiting for a train, or any other time I get a spare moment. It's good to see everything you have to know down on a few cards, rather than on millions of scrappy sheets in a folder.

The second is a comment by a **visual** and **auditory** learner. Note how Doris uses visual methods to create the Mind Map™ but auditory methods in the form of mnemonics to recall it.

CASE STUDY – EXAM MIND MAP™ CREATED BY DORIS

This Mind Map™ (Figure 9.1) is specifically related to memory strategies and recall. There are five traits that I needed to memorise with a number of factors related to each of those traits. NEO AGRI CONSCIENTIOUS-NESS is a mnemonic for the five traits. The more connections I make with a piece of information, the easier it is to recall and the connection I made here was that new agriculture is conscientious.

The same goes for AGREEABLENESS. I saw a film called *I Am Sam* in which Sean Penn plays a person who has learning difficulties who is fighting for custody of his daughter and embodies the factors of the traits in the character he is playing. If I split this Mind Map™ over three pages so that when printed the Mind Map™ was easy to see, I would have a number at the top of the page to indicate how many sections I would have on each page. This would then give me a number I could memorise, so if I had two sections on each page, the number would be 222. So in an exam I would remember the number, visualise the pictures and then the picture would prompt the mnemonic.

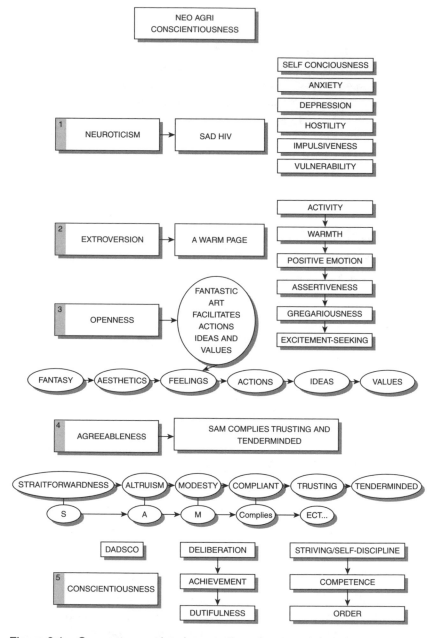

Figure 9.1   Concept map showing creation of personal acronyms as mnemonic to revise psychological terms

Practising sample examination questions under timed conditions

It is crucial to obtain a **bank of sample questions or past examination papers** during the revision period. When you feel that you have revised your work as well as you can, select questions from the bank or from previous papers to answer. It is important to practise questions under the same conditions (exact times) as those you will face in the exam. This exam preparation is one of the most important steps in giving you **confidence to actually do the exam**.

When looking at previous exam papers **look carefully at the rubric** (instructions to the candidate printed at the top of the examination paper) printed on the front of the paper and under the section headings. Many students have left examinations only to find out later that they did not do a compulsory question. The rubric tells you **how many questions you have to answer in each section, and how long you have to do the paper.** If, for example, you are doing a 3-hour paper and have a 25% extension, you will have 225 minutes. So, for example, if you have to answer four **equal value** questions, your time could be spent as follows:

- 10–15 minutes to select your questions   15
- For each question:

  - 5 minutes planning   20
  - 40 minutes writing   160
  - 7 minutes proofreading   30

However, if one question is worth 50% of the marks, give it half the time, and split the remainder among the other questions.

All papers require a different distribution of time. If you look at previous papers and practise questions in the time allocated, you will have rehearsed for the examination.

When you have chosen the questions you have decided to practise you should go through the **stages of essay planning**, which have been outlined in Chapter 5. By now you should be able to do this automatically (type of question, type of answer, key words, general issues, theme, plan, and essay). If possible, get somebody to read your practice essays and give you feedback. If this is not possible, at least you know that you have managed to complete the required essays in the time available for the examination.

The day before the exam

- Set your alarm to get up at the same time as you want to be up tomorrow.
- Don't look at new material.
- Have a general run through of index cards/Mind Maps™.
- Do some light exercise.
- Drink water and eat healthy food.
- Go to bed at a reasonable time. Don't stay up late studying the night before the examination and skip breakfast or lunch just before the exam to do last-minute revision. This form of cramming is dangerous in two ways:

  - First, you will not remember work you have crammed just before the exam, as it will not have gone into your long-term memory.
  - Secondly, last-minute cramming causes anxiety, and that is not the best mindset in which to take the examination.

- Pack materials for the next day:

  - Several pens and pencils, ruler, eraser etc.
  - A trustworthy watch.
  - If you are using a calculator, take spare batteries.
  - A bottle of water and banana, sweets, glucose tablets.
  - A jumper in case you get cold sitting still for so long.

Sitting the exam

After all this excellent revision and preparation you should have little to worry about.

The final preparations, and those which should ensure that you will be successful, are **to be well rested, well fed, calm and confident**.

Be rested

Fatigue is a danger in examinations, as you will not be working at your greatest potential and recent research has shown that lack of sleep can affect general intelligence.

Recent newspaper articles suggest that people trying to memorise facts and sitting for exams should take brief naps as part of their preparation. If you have to sit more than one exam in a day try to have a short 'power nap' between them. Even a few minutes' sleep can help to recharge your batteries.

Be well fed

Failing to eat before exams can cause you to have low blood sugar levels and this may make you feel weak and drowsy. **Eat a nutritious meal at least an hour before you take the exam** so that your body is at its peak, and can support you to perform at your best. If you are taking a long examination, you may wish to take **some dried fruit such as apricots or figs to eat or some still water to drink. Make sure you check that this is allowed under the examination rules at your institution**. If bottles of water are not allowed and the weather is very hot, glasses of water should be made available on request.

Be calm and confident

You should aim to walk into the exam room feeling calm, confident and alert. If you are feeling anxious, try some deep breathing exercises or Brain Gym® (Dennison). If it's a nice day, get off the bus two stops early and walk to college.

During the exam

Regardless of what happens always remain calm and don't become distracted or upset by external problems of any kind. Concentrate on the task.

- Read the rubric (general instructions) carefully.
- Read the whole paper and decide on your choice of questions. Read each question twice.
- Interpret the questions.
- Consider all key words. Highlight them if you wish.
- Allocate your time according to the number of questions to be answered and the mark value ascribed to each question. Allow time to proofread your answer to each question. Use this time to check spellings, cross out notes or drafts and that you have numbered the answer correctly.
- Always answer your best questions first or second in your time allocations to maximise your results.
- Plan your answers and use your time.
- Keep writing.

Strategies to try if your mind goes blank

- Try a relaxation exercise, deep breathing or thinking something pleasant.
- Try writing out the question and ask yourself questions about it. Start simple (Who? What? Why? When? Where? and How?). Now try some more difficult questions.
- Brainstorm a concept map or write key words.
- If you can't remember something when writing, leave a blank in case it comes to you later.
- If all this fails, go to the bathroom and splash water on your face and go back in and try again.
- Don't leave early. Sit there and get through it.

POINTS TO REMEMBER

In preparing for examinations:

- adopt the right mindset;
- make preparations with your institution – Student Services, Assessment Unit;
- plan your revision and compile timetables both for the revision period and for the examination period;
- revise using the most appropriate methods for your cognitive and learning style;
- practise sample examination questions using the methods used in Chapter 5 if essays are required;
- check that you know the date, time and room of the exam;
- read the whole paper carefully;
- allocate your time;
- use your time wisely.

10 Using Role Play

Paula Dawson

This chapter:

- illustrates how you can put your knowledge into practice through role play;
- suggests activities to prepare for and follow up from role play;
- helps you to think about how role play can be useful for you;
- explores how role play can be used to develop your practical skills.

Introduction

Role play is an effective method of learning, particularly for students on **practical courses and placements**. Through role play you can put your knowledge into practice and develop practical skills, which will enable you to gain confidence. The skills and strategies learnt can then be **transferred to the professional context**, not only while you are studying, but in future employment. Role play can also be useful for students not on practical courses. For example, it can be **a valuable way of preparing for presentations and interviews**.

This chapter demonstrates the use of role play in a certain context – in this instance, on a placement as a dietician. By its very nature role play lends itself to be explained though a specific example. Discussion on how role play can be used in other contexts, such as teaching, will be given towards the end of the chapter. You may well be able to **apply the ideas to your course of study**.

Before you begin, think about **what your goals are and what you are aiming to achieve**. Think about the particular skills that you would like to develop. With this in mind, see how you can incorporate role play into your learning.

CASE STUDY

Mira was studying Human Nutrition and Dietetics and had completed all the written aspects of her course, but had failed her first placement. Being dyslexic, Mira found that she was slow at completing practical tasks and that she had difficulty doing many tasks at the same time, particularly under pressure and time constraints. Mira wanted to improve her skills and be equipped with strategies to help overcome her difficulties, and ultimately pass her course.

As a dietician, Mira was required to know a lot of detailed information, such as the breakdown of foods, serving sizes, and biochemistry. It was essential that she could access this information from memory when seeing clients.

Mira's main difficulties were with remembering what to ask a client during consultation, while at the same time calculating calories according to food portions, and maintaining eye contact. She would often 'lose track' of what question she was going to ask next. She was also concerned about her slowness at these tasks, and the need to appear confident and professional. After the consultation, Mira would be required to enter the client information on a record card, which also gave her cause for concern as she had difficulty with correctly ordering the information. Above all, since having failed her placement, she lacked self-confidence.

After discussing what her main areas of need were, Mira and her tutor decided that a useful way to develop the skills necessary for her intended profession and to practise 'being a dietician' would be through role play.

They simulated consultations with 'clients' (tutor) with different medical conditions so that Mira could have practice in a variety of situations.

(Continued)

(Continued)

This was supplemented with pre- and follow-up activities, such as filling out record cards after the 'consultation'.

Applying what she had learnt on her course to real-life situations helped Mira to develop her skills and demonstrate her knowledge, which in turn helped greatly to rebuild her confidence and pass the placement.

Here are some suggestions that Mira found worked for her.

Preparation

Read through the client's previous record notes and jot down key points onto a pad in the correct order (for example, date order with the most recent information first). Ask yourself questions: what is this person's medical history? What information do I already know? What do I need to find out? What questions am I going to ask, and in what order?

If this is the client's first consultation and there are no previous record notes, you might like to **draw up a checklist** on a piece of card so that you can enter essential information onto it. Take this into the consultation to help you remember what information you need to find out. Figure 10.1 provides an example of a general checklist.

You might like **to make up a series of cards** for different medical conditions where more specific information is needed. **The cards could be colour coded** and you could use pictures to illustrate them.

You could try using other colour coded cards to help you remember what questions you may need to ask. For example, if you need to find

Age: _____

Weight: _____

Height: _____

BMI (Body Mass Index): _____

Additional information:

_____

_____

_____

_____

_____

_____

Figure 10.1   Patient checklist

out a client's diet history, you could write down what you need to ask (in order) onto a card, such as in Figure 10.2. **Visual association can help to aid recall, so it may be helpful to draw diagrams linked to your questions**. After a while, you might find that you don't need to use the cards all the time, as you are able to remember each question by visualising the associated picture.

Using a personal organiser (see Chapter 11) can be helpful, not only for organising your time and workload, but also for storing important information. Among other things, Mira included in her personal organiser a list of food portion sizes, which she needed in order to calculate calories and suggest meal plans for clients.

1.	**First meal of the day:** _____
	_____
2.	**Anything before lunch?** _____
	_____
3.	**Lunch:** _____
	_____
4.	**Anything before dinner?** _____
	_____
5.	**Dinner:** _____
	_____
6.	**Anything else?** _____

Figure 10.2   Daily food intake

Using a case study as a basis for your role play

As you are trying to practise being in a real-life situation, why not try **using real-life case studies?** The internet is a useful resource for this, and you can find Question and Answer (Q&A) pages where people have written in to get advice from doctors and health professionals, or you may have case studies in your course books. **Case studies provide good, real examples**, which you can use as a basis for your role play.

Alternatively, **try using an internet search engine** to find an article on a particular subject, for example Crohn's disease. This can be good reading practice for you too. Try skim-reading the article, highlighting key words and/or jotting down key words or sentences onto a piece of paper. (For more reading strategies, see Chapter 4.) Then, think about what information you would need to find out from a client with Crohn's disease. You may like to use a checklist as suggested above to help you.

See what you can find – be creative!

Rehearsing your role play

The next step is to put **all your preparation into practice** in a role play. You could try this with your learning support tutor, friend, family member or classmate.

Your **role play partner can assume the role of the patient or client**, with whatever illness or medical condition you choose. Try a variety to test your knowledge – an overweight, middle-aged man with heart problems, a pregnant woman, a person with diabetes, or an older person with malnutrition.

It is important to relax, so try doing some relaxation exercises before you begin, such as closing your eyes and taking deep breaths. Relax the muscles in your body, relax your shoulders and imagine that your body feels heavy and warm. Don't worry about making mistakes – learning is all about 'trial and error'!

Assume your role, and remember to be professional as you are trying to mirror a real-life situation. Use your checklists to help you remember what you need to ask. As you go along, **make notes** onto your checklist card or a notepad. If you need to calculate calories, do this at the end so that you do not lose track of the questions you are asking. Next, **discuss with your client** what you have found out from their answers. Try giving them advice and recommendations. For example, if your client is an overweight, middle-aged male, try suggesting ways that he can lower his calorie intake. This would be a useful way to demonstrate your expertise.

Follow-up activities

A **useful follow-up exercise** could be to suggest a meal plan for the client. You could write down a meal plan for a week of a healthier diet and give this to them, explaining the reasons for your recommendations. Practise doing calorie calculations for this also.

Then fill out the client's record card with your notes from the consultation. If this is the client's first record card, enter their general details (age, weight, height, BMI) in first at the top of the card. Use your checklists to help you.

Other uses of role play

- As mentioned earlier, role play is **particularly useful for students on practical courses and placements**, such as dieticians, doctors, nurses, social workers, engineers, teachers, etc. If you are training to be a teacher, for example, think of how you could incorporate role play into the classroom. In a history lesson, students could have great fun **acting out scenes in history**, or pretending to be a prime minister giving an historical speech. In English lessons, students can take on the **roles of characters in novels and plays** and be asked questions by the class about their reasons for certain actions.
- In order to monitor how you come across to your pupils in your role as a teacher, it can be useful to **tape record yourself when you are in the classroom**. Take note of the **tone and pitch of your voice** – what effect does it have on the students in the class? Is your speech calm, clear and even? What is your rate of speech – are you talking too quickly? Are you easy to understand? If you **videotape yourself giving a lesson**, notice your pupils' reactions to what you are saying. Are they responding positively? What things could you do to improve?
- Role play is an **integral part of learning a new language**. Try **acting out different scenarios** such as ordering food from a restaurant, buying train tickets, and introducing yourself at a party. Think about your intonation and pronunciation as well.
- If you are not on a practice-based course, think of how role play can be useful for you. Often, **'doing it'** is a great way to learn. If you need to give a

presentation, rehearse this in front of someone, such as a family member. If you are going for a **job interview, try role playing** this with someone. Ask them to **give you feedback** on what went well, and what you need to develop. Why not try **explaining a concept** to a friend, family member or classmate? Talk it through with them. Not only will this help you to demonstrate your knowledge, but they might learn something new also!

* As well as getting feedback from others, you could try **videotaping yourself giving a presentation** or acting out a scenario. It can be a bit unnerving seeing yourself on camera at first, but it does provide a good opportunity to see yourself from a different perspective. **Take note of your body language** – do you pace back and forth? Do you keep touching your hair? Take a look at your posture – are you standing up straight or slouching? Does your body look closed or open? Often people don't notice this until they see themselves doing it. Do you keep reading your presentation from a laptop or cards? **Are you making eye-contact with your audience**? If you are acting out a scenario with a partner, take note of how you interact with them.

POINTS TO REMEMBER

* Think about how you can incorporate role play into your learning.
* Try to make it as real as possible.
* Relax and don't worry about making mistakes.
* Prepare for your role play and try some follow-up activities.
* Use materials or aids if helpful.

11 How ICT Can Help You

John Brennan

This chapter:

- surveys the hardware and software typically provided by the Disabled Students' Allowance (DSA) and equivalent free alternatives for those without the DSA;
- helps you make best use of the technology provided;
- helps you avoid some common pitfalls;
- links the technology to the strategies provided earlier in this book;
- emphasises the importance of training to become adept at using the technology with indications of where to find help and information.

As there are many links to training and exercise material on the World Wide Web, **it is highly recommended that students take advantage of the internet**.

Key

- *Format > Styles*   means select the named key or menu item followed by the next key or menu item.
- *Ctrl + S*   means press both keys simultaneously.
- *Ctrl + Alt + Del*   means press all three keys simultaneously.

Who needs ICT?

The software made available under the DSA can be used effectively by all students; not just by dyslexic students. Anybody writing an essay, report or case study will make good use of a word processor; anybody working with numbers can use a spreadsheet. Even the specialist software that is targeted at dyslexics, such as TextHELP Read & Write Gold, Inspiration and Dragon Naturally Speaking, can and is used by students and others who have no problems with reading and writing. Two of these software packages attempt, with considerable success, to turn reading into listening and writing into speaking. They are, to some extent, supporting a learning style as much as overcoming or bypassing a dyslexic problem.

Such transpositions require some effort and discipline on the part of the user, but this is true of all software. Although modern software is much more intuitive than in the past, and software allows the user many ways to get to the right result, **all software requires the user to make some modification to their working methods** if all the full benefits of the software are to be gained; hence the need for training, and the emphasis given to it in this chapter.

Moreover, and apologies for the truism, computers work best with digital material. Modern hardware and software can convert analogue input – voice, print or graphic – into its digital counterparts but it takes time, knowledge and effort, and will not be perfect. Help to cut out this intermediate stage **by convincing your tutors and lecturers to make their handouts available in electronic format**.

What is available?

Computer hardware

The computer made available will usually be a Windows PC, though students in so-called creative courses may be offered a Macintosh.

Despite the fervour of the zealots of both platforms, they are more similar than they are different, and most software is available for both.

(It assumed that if you use UNIX or Linux, you know more than enough about IT.)

No distinction is made between desktop computers and portables in this chapter. Note that the use of a portable, or, indeed, any form of personal digital assistant (PDA) in a seminar, lecture or other communal learning environment can be disruptive to the other participants. **You should remember to ask permission**.

Other hardware

Scanners
As well as page scanners there are portable scanners (reading pens) which enable information such as references or quotes to be stored digitally for later transfer to a computer. More expensive versions contain built-in text-to-speech software and dictionaries and can read aloud scanned-in text to help develop vocabulary skills.

Microphones
If you are intending to use speech recognition software, **make sure you have a good quality microphone**; if you intend to use Dragon Naturally Speaking, **make sure you have a compatible microphone**.

http://support.nuance.com/compatibility/default.asp

Digital recorders
Digital voice recorders can be used to record lectures, seminars or one's own notes (preferably not in the library), or for dictating essays and reports. Recordings can be transferred to personal music players for review or revision, or can be input to speech recognition software. Again if you intend to use Dragon Naturally Speaking, **make sure you have a compatible recorder**.

http://support.nuance.com/compatibility/default.asp

Personal digital assistants (PDAs)

A PDA is a portable, personal electronic organiser; a combination of diary, notebook, address book, alarm clock, voice recorder, music player and mobile phone. They can help to manage some of the organisational difficulties associated with dyslexia. Note that the more features they have, **the bigger, more expensive and more difficult to learn to use they will be** – much of this functionality is already on your computer. **How important is portability**? If buying one for recording, make sure it is compatible with your software.

Spellcheckers

All word processors have a spellchecker, but you can also get a standalone, portable spell checker or thesaurus. Most include a speech function that lets you hear the spelling suggestion or definition. Again, **how important is portability**?

USB memory sticks

USB (Universal Serial Bus) memory sticks are extremely useful as a means of moving data around, say, between home and university. Though, **try not to rely on them as a form of backup**.

Additional hardware

You will also need a printer and, possibly, speakers. You needn't be extravagant.

Software

Operating systems

Both Microsoft Windows and Apple Macintosh offer facilities to the dyslexic student to change and improve the computer/user interface. Severely disabled users can substitute voice commands for the keyboard and mouse, and have the computer read text displayed on the screen. Less dramatic changes can be made to the screen resolution, colours and fonts.

If, for example, black text on a white background in Microsoft Word causes problems, it is very simple to change the background. In Windows click the *mouse right button (in a standard set-up) > Properties* to reveal the Display Properties dialogue box.

Select the Appearance tab, and then *Advanced* (at the bottom) to reveal the Advanced Appearance dialogue box. In the *Item: scroll box* hit the scroll button (⌄), *and select Window,* then by using the *Color 1: control* button pick a new colour or click *Other* for a greater range of colours and shades (light to dark). Use both controls and, when happy, note the Hue, Saturation, Luminescence and RGB numbers if you wish to change *other* elements (such as the Desktop) in Windows or other programs. Click *OK*.

Two additional points:

- **Don't be afraid to experiment**; there is always a way to get back to the default setting.
- In Windows **use the right mouse button** to get a set of options; frequently this will jog the memory enough for you to find what you want to do.

Both Microsoft and Apple provide help on all their accessibility features.

www.microsoft.com/enable/products/windowsxp/default.aspx

www.apple.com/support/tiger/voiceover/

In addition the operating system will include some basic PDA tools such as a note taker, calendar, recorder and paint program. More importantly they incorporate a web browser and email client. **Explore the operating system**; what you want may already be there.

Computer maintenance software
To keep your computer running well it will need, like all machines, to be maintained. The operating system will have much of this functionality embedded within it – the user needs to know how and when to use it.

Computer maintenance will include:

- Updating the operating system itself. Windows has become notorious for the number of emergency patches it requires.
- Adding and removing software programs.
- Removing redundant data and temporary files.
- Defragmenting the hard disk.

All these tiresome, yet necessary tasks can be automated. In Windows, use the *Start > Control Panel* and *Administrative Tools* menus to set up the necessary options.

Most important of all **you must protect your computer from malicious interference** from the internet. This means installing and running a firewall, anti-virus software and spyware removal software. Both Microsoft Windows and Macs have anti-virus and firewall components. There are commercial products, and there are free products available for download from the internet.

   www.techsupportalert.com/best-46_free_utilities.htm#5

Application software
There is, of course, an enormous amount of application software available to assist users in their work.

For those who are not entitled to the DSA, or are awaiting it, there are many free alternatives available. Some students may require some course specific software; an example might be those following a media or arts course. Again there are many free alternatives.

   http://sourceforge.net/

What can you do with ICT?

Academic tasks
ICT is useful for both completing assignments – brainstorming with Inspiration or analysing statistics with Excel or researching on the internet – and 'polishing' the work before submission. It is sometimes a

temptation to spend more time on form rather than content. **Try to resist this**.

Nevertheless, as illustrated in Table 11.1, ICT can help dyslexic students with all the academic tasks covered in the previous chapters of this book. In some instances you are directed towards related files for each chapter on the CD-ROM.

General tips

As I have mentioned before **don't be afraid to experiment**. When there is some spare time available, try something new. For example, try to import a picture into your essay or reflection or try to present a column of numbers in Excel into a graph.

Don't panic

Of course it is easier to experiment if one can be sure that nothing can go wrong. That is not always possible, since it is by making mistakes that we learn, but it is possible to limit the resulting damage. The most common form of panic is caused by losing work. This can be caused by different forms of failure: hardware; software; and, most common of all, human.

To prevent, or, at least, limit the effects of hardware failure **take backups of your data.** This means regularly (every day, certainly every week) copying your data files onto:

- Another part of the hard drive (Poor).
- Another drive in the same computer (Better).
- A removable drive (Best). As virtually all modern computers have a CD-ROM writer (if not a DVD writer) together with CD writing software, this is easy. **Remember that CD (re) writable discs are cheap compared to your time and effort.** A USB memory stick should only be used as a temporary store, not as a backup device. Universities will also provide network drives which are backed up daily. As there will be a storage limit, **use them for your essential files.**

Table 11.1   ICT tools for academic tasks

	Tasks	Tools
Managing your Workload	Planners (Week, Term, Semester, Year) **(GO to CD-ROM)**	Word Excel
	To do lists **(GO to CD-ROM)**	Word
Understanding Your Preferred Learning Style	Use the internet shortcut on the CD-ROM to give you an indication of your preferred learning style. **(GO to CD-ROM)**	
Visual	Use graphical tools (Paint.NET, Word, Inspiration 8) as the means to express and clarify your ideas, your notes and your revision.	
Auditory	Use audio hardware (microphones, recorders, players) and software (Dragon, TextHELP) to transform text to sound.	
Kinaesthetic	… mmmmm …	
Note Taking and Note Making	Note taking **(GO to CD-ROM)**	Digital recorders
	Note making **(Go to CD-ROM)**	Word Inspiration 8
Reading Strategies and Speed Reading	Reading for meaning Research Revision	ABBYY FineReader TextHELP
Answering Essay Questions	Structuring the essay	Inspiration 8
	Writing the Essay **(Go to CD-ROM)**	Word
Structuring Different Writing Genres	As above.	
Improving Your Grammar, Spelling and Punctuation	Writing	Word Spelling and Grammar Word Thesaurus Wordweb
	Mnemonics Computation Statistics	Word Paint.NET Excel

(Continued)

Table 11.1   (Continued)

	Tasks	Tools
Mathematic Skills and Using Statistics	Shapes **(Go to CD-ROM)**	Word Paint.NET
	Tables	Excel
Examination Techniques	Visual revision methods	Word Inspiration 8 Paint.NET
	Auditory revision techniques	Digital recorders Players TextHELP
	Relaxation techniques **(GO to CD-ROM)**	Word
Using Role Play	Scripts	Word

Much more often it is us, the human operator, making a mistake that is the problem. Since we cannot eliminate mistakes, we should try to reduce their number and their severity. The key words are **organisation** and **good habits.**

Organisation

Keep a track of your data files by **organising them into folders and subfolders. Use as many levels as you need**. Organise by module, assignment and element of work. **Use meaningful titles** for your folders and files.

Keeping your hard disk organised will make taking backups easier, will make it less likely you lose data and facilitate transporting data between computers at home and college or workplace.

Good habits

When editing a piece of work, such as a document in Word, a spreadsheet in Excel or a presentation in PowerPoint, make sure you get into the habit of **saving it under a different name**. I just use an incremental number – ICT For Dyslexics #1.doc, ICT For Dyslexics #2.doc, etc. Use the File > Save As dialogue.

Get into the habit of **saving your work frequently**, say every time you pause typing. It's easy: *Ctrl + S key* combination (see below).

Set up the *Save AutoRecover info every:* box to **5 or 10 minutes**. This is accessed via the *Tools > Options* menu. If there is a power failure or software crash, it will enable you to recover some of the information input since the last time the document was saved.

Finally when you do make a mistake, don't try to correct the mistake; **undo it and try again.** Use the *Ctrl + Z* key combination (see below). It is usually easier to go back to the beginning and try again.

General advice
As mentioned before, and if using a PC, **click the right button** on the mouse to give yourself a short menu of options. In Word I use this to get synonyms or when I want to format a line or table.

Learn to use some keyboard shortcuts. These are activated by simultaneously pressing on the Ctrl, Windows or Alt key with one (usu-ally) or more other keys. There are a large number of these, and It is impossible to remember them all, but a select few will save you time and effort. Some of the best are:

- *Alt + Tab*   Switch between open programs
- *Alt + underlined letter in menu*   Opens the menu
- *Ctrl + C*   Copy
- *Ctrl + X*   Cut
- *Ctrl + V*   Paste
- *Ctrl + Y*   Repeat the last action
- *Ctrl + Z*   Undo
- *Ctrl + S*   Save
- *Ctrl + Print Screen*   Copies the screen to the clipboard
- *Ctrl + Alt + Print Screen*   Copies the active window to
                                                        the clipboard
- *Windows Logo*   Start menu
- *Windows Logo + R*   Run dialogue box
- *Windows Logo + E*   Windows Explorer
- *Windows Logo + F*   Find files or folders

A full list can be found at:

http://support.microsoft.com/default.aspx?scid=kb;en-us;q126449

⊚ (GO to Internet Shortcut on CD-ROM)

Microsoft Word
As the word processor is probably the most used of all programs used at college, university or work, it is worth while to make a special effort to learn how to use this software. For example, Word is an extremely sophisticated piece of software and it is a mistake to treat it as an old-fashioned typewriter. **Learn to apply properties** (like font, colour or where it is to appear on the page) **to objects** (see Figure 11.1).

Objects		Properties
Paragraphs		Font
Titles		Paragraph
Bullets & Lists	Apply	Tabs
Headings		Borders
Headers & Footers		Language
Tables		Numbering

Figure 11.1   Applying properties to objects in Microsoft Word

Use the Styles and Formatting task pane to choose, modify and apply styles to the objects in your document. **Experiment!** The pane is called up from the *Format > Styles and Formatting ...* menu item.

Another example of Word's rich functionality which is rarely recognised by its users and is regularly required by students is the ability to draw diagrams. These could be process control diagrams, organisational charts or flowcharts.

These can be inserted into one's document using the *Insert > Picture > AutoShapes tab*. With this, one can insert lines, arrows and shapes to build up a diagram. An example of a flowchart is included on the CD-ROM.

⊙ (GO to Flowchart Template on CD-ROM)

When manipulating objects in a diagram, or files in a folder remember that

- **holding down the CTRL key while pointing and clicking will select individual objects;**
- **holding down the Shift key while pointing and clicking, or pointing and dragging will select a range of objects.**

Diagrams can also be drawn using your mind-mapping software. If you are likely to be drawing a lot of complicated diagrams, it may be worth while investing in a dedicated program, such as this free one:

www.freeserifsoftware.com/software/DrawPlus/default.asp

Help

By far the most important tip I can give you is to **get trained** in the hardware and software you have. The DSA will usually provide training in the supplied hardware and software. Unfortunately this will be provided in halfday or day sessions, and it is very difficult to absorb new information over such a long period. It is much more useful to have short hour or hour and a half training sessions. Inevitably it will be up to you to **teach yourself**.

The good news is that there are many free sources of information. I will use Word as an example, but all the DSA supplied software and hardware will have similar sources of information.

The different sources are:

Microsoft Word Help

Microsoft Word Help (called up by Function F1) provides a wealth of information. One can use the Office Assistant, which attempts to provide a helpful intermediary between the user and the help database, or not. It is a matter of taste, but many find the Office Assistant more irritating than helpful.

Turn it off by *Help > Show the Office Assistant > Right click the assistant > Options > Uncheck the box.*

Without the Office Assistant there are three ways to use the help database:

- Contents
- Answer Wizard
- Index.

If you don't know exactly what you are looking for, **ask the Answer Wizard**; if you do, **look up the Index** and if you are somewhere in the middle, **browse the Contents**.

Wizards

Some software programs provide wizards to help the user. A wizard is a structured dialogue in which the user is prompted for responses until all the necessary parameters are set. **Use them if they are helpful**; some are better than others.

Manuals

Many software suppliers now either do not supply manuals, or only supply extremely slim volumes intended merely to get one started; some only provide them on the internet. For example:

www.inspiration.com/tutorials/index.cfm?fuseaction=insp

(⊙) **(GO to Inspiration Quick Start Tutorial on CD-ROM)**

Third parties also offer manuals on the internet for the student to download.

www.ebitsolutions.net/services/resources/free_training_manuals.htm

The internet offers software suppliers a cheaper, more updatable mechanism to deliver their user documentation than the printed page. **Yet another reason to get broadband internet access!**

Supplier websites

All software suppliers have websites, which are often accessed from the Help tab, as shown. They will offer documentation and, in some cases, downloads. The Microsoft Office support site is a particularly rich resource.

http://office.microsoft.com/en-gb/default.aspx

When browsing a support website, or any website for that matter, use the **skimming** and **scanning** techniques introduced in Chapter 4 to find relevant information. The **frequently asked questions (FAQs)** section can often supply the answer one is looking for.

User communities

In addition to the supplier websites there are a lot of unofficial, or semi-official, software and technology forums on the Web. These also can provide much useful information. Two examples are:

www.oooforum.org/forum/

www.voicerecognition.com/board/

Searching the internet

Although I have provided some website addresses (technically URI/URL = Universal Resource Identifier/Locator), it is not a complete list. As the internet is a dynamic resource with new websites appearing and current websites disappearing or changing on a daily basis, providing a fixed directory seems a futile exercise. It is much better for you, the student, to **find the resource when you need it**, and to do this you need to search.

Use Google, unless you can think of a good reason not to.

Learn to refine your search:

• Use either the advanced search options link; or
• search within results (at the bottom of the page) to limit the next search to the websites already selected.

Practise! When you have found a website that is useful, now or in the future, **add it to your favourites** (Internet Explorer) or bookmarks (Mozilla). **Organise your favourites and bookmarks** in the same way as folders and files.

POINTS TO REMEMBER

• Get Broadband if possible, and use the internet to get help.
• Use the right mouse button (when using Windows machines) to get the first level of help.
• Explore your computer, and learn.
• Don't panic. You will always be asked to confirm any action that may be disastrous.

Glossary

Abbreviation Shortening something by omitting parts of it.

Abstract A summary of the main points of an argument or theory.

Acronyms A word formed from the initial letters of a multi-word name.

AlphaSmart A portable computer keyboard which you can use and then download to a PC.

Amanuensis Someone skilled in the transcription of speech (especially dictation).

Analytic Using or skilled in using analysis (i.e. separating a whole – intellectual or substantial – into its elemental parts or basic principles).

Argumentative Given to or characterised by argument; 'an argumentative discourse'.

Articulating Uttering distinct syllables or words.

Auditory Of or relating to the process of hearing; 'auditory processing'.

Bibliography Alphabetical reference list at end of an essay or coursework.

Bottom up Looking at something analytically rather than holistically.

Brainstorming Thinking intensely about a topic or theme and recoding the ideas.

Citation A short note acknowledging a source of information or quoting a passage.

Chunking Grouping together in compact sections.

Clause An expression including a subject and verb but not constituting a complete sentence.

Cognitive style Thinking style.

Concept mapping A map of abstract or general ideas inferred or derived from specific instances.

Concrete materials Capable of being perceived by the senses; not abstract or imaginary.

Condensing Reducing or compacting.

Deadline The point in time at which something must be completed.

Endnote Footnote at the end of a chapter or section.

Errors Inadvertent incorrectness.

Evaluative Appraising; exercising or involving careful evaluations.

Explanatory Serving or intended to explain or make clear.

Expository Serving to expound or set forth.

Footnote A note placed below the text on a printed page.

Genre A style of expressing yourself in writing.

Grasshopper One who looks at issues holistically.

Holistic Emphasising the organic or functional relation between parts and the whole.

HTML Hyper Text Mark-up Language.

Illustrations A visual representation (a picture or diagram) that is used to make some subject more pleasing or easier to understand.

Imagery The ability to form mental images of things or events; usually related to the senses.

Inchworm A thinking process which moves analytically from the bottom up.

Index cards Coloured cards which can be used to store information and sorted in different ways.

Information processing Thinking about information and organising it.

Integers Numbers.

Interactive Capable of acting on or influencing each other.

Interpretative To make sense of or assign a meaning to.

Kinaesthetic Of or relating to the process of movement; 'kinaesthetic processing'. A 'hands-on' approach to things.

Learning style The way one learns.

Linear notes Notes which are kept in sequential lines rather than patterns.

Listening comprehension An ability to understand the meaning or importance of something (or the knowledge acquired as a result); through listening.

Literature review A review of the books available on a specific topic.

Memory pegs A set or group of thoughts which trigger other thoughts.

Metacognitive Knowing how you think.

Methodology The system of methods followed in a particular discipline.

Mind mapping Term coined by Tony Buzan to indicate the grouping of concepts relating to a topic.

Mnemonics A method or system for improving the memory.

Morphology The structure of words.

Multi-sensory Using more than one sense.

Object The noun or pronoun after a verb or preposition.

Overview A holistic view of the whole work.

Passive The voice used to indicate that the subject of the verb is the recipient (not the source) of the action denoted by the verb.

PDA Personal digital assistant.

PDF Portable Document Format – Adobe Acrobat.

PEST/STEP Political, Economic, Social and Technological aspects of a subject.

Plagiarism Use of another person's ideas or findings as your own by simply copying them and reproducing them without due acknowledgement.

PowerPoint projection The projection of a presentation from a computer onto a screen made in PowerPoint.

Phonetics Relating to the scientific study of speech sounds.

Phonology The study of the sound system of a given language and the analysis and classification of its phonemes.

Prioritise Assign a priority to.

Prioritised reading list Reading lists in which the most important books are clearly indicated.

Punctuation The use of certain marks to clarify meaning of written material by grouping words grammatically into sentences and clauses and phrases.

Q Notes A way of taking notes suggested by Jim Bourke, in which a question is asked and an answer provided.

Questionnaire A form containing a set of questions; submitted to people in order to gain statistical information.

Reading comprehension An ability to understand the meaning or importance of something (or the knowledge acquired as a result) through reading.

Referencing Acknowledgement of a source of information.

Role play The rehearsal of a specific scenario.

Roots Square root – number which when multiplied by itself equals a given number. Cube root – a number which when multiplied three times equals a given number.

Rubric A heading that is printed in red or in a special type. The overall instructions on exam papers.

Sans serif A font style which is plain and without loops.

Scheduled Planned or scheduled for some certain time or times; 'the scheduled lectures'.

Semester One of two divisions of an academic year. Half a year; a period of six months.

Sigma The sum of a set of numbers.

Simultaneously At the same time.

Squared A number multiplied by itself.

Standard deviation Statistical measure of spread or variability.

Statistics A branch of applied mathematics concerned with the collection and interpretation of quantitative data and the use of probability theory to estimate population parameters.

Strategies Systematic plans of action.

Subject The noun or pronoun before the verb.

Sub-vocalising To verbalise silently.

SWOT Strengths, Weaknesses, Opportunities and Threats.

Techniques A practical method applied to some particular task.

Template A model or standard for making comparisons.

Top down Looking at things holistically, from the top.

Trigger (memory) Any thought that sets in motion a range of other thoughts.

Unpacking the question Methods of making the question easier to understand. Analysing it in sections.

URL Universal Resource Locator (letters you write in the bar after www. to locate a website).

Verbalising To think or express in words.

Visual Relating to or using sight; 'visual powers'; 'visual navigation'. Able to be seen; 'a visual presentation'; 'a visual image'.

Visualising Thinking in visual images.

Viva (Voice) An examination where questions are asked and answered orally rather than a written paper.

References and further reading

If you have found this book helpful, you might also find other similar books useful. As a start you could try the following books, many of which were referred to in this volume. In addition, there is a list of websites that might also be of interest.

Burke, J. (2002) *Tools for Thought*. Portsmouth, NH: Heinemann.

Burns, T. and Sinfield, S. (2002) *Essential Study Skills*. London: SAGE Publications.

Buzan, T. (1988) *Make the Most of Your Mind* (rev. edition). London: Pan Books.

Buzan, T. (1995) *Use Your Head* (4th edition). London: BBC.

Buzan, T. (2004) *The Speed Reading Book*. London: BBC.

Buzan, T. and Buzan, B. (2006) *The Mind Map Book* (rev. edition). London: BBC Active.

Chambers, P. and Tovey, M. (2004) *Radiant Thinking Skills*. Bucknell: Learning Technologies Ltd.

Chinn, S. J. and Ashcroft, J. R. (1998) *Mathematics for Dyslexics: A Teaching Handbook* (2nd edition). London: Whurr.

Cottrell, S. (2003) *The Study Skills Handbook* (2nd edition). Basingstoke: Palgrave Macmillan.

Creme, P. (2000) 'The "personal" in university writing: uses of reflective learning journals', in M. R. Lea and B. Stierer (eds) *Student Writing in Higher Education: New Contexts*. Buckingham: The Society for Research in Higher Education/Open University Press.

Dennison, P. (1994) *Switching On: The Whole Brain Answer to Dyslexia*. Ventura, CA: Edu-Kinesthetics Inc.

Dennison, P. and Dennison, G. (1992) *Brain Gym: Simple Activities for Whole Brain Learning*. Ventura, CA: Edu-Kinesthetics Inc.

Dennison, P. and Dennison, G. (1994) *Brain Gym: Teacher's Edition Revised*. Ventura, CA: Edu-Kinesthetics Inc.

Dennison, P. and Dennison, G. (1995) *Educational Kinesiology In-Depth: The Seven Dimensions of Intelligence*. Ventura, CA: Edu-Kinesthetics Inc.

Gilroy, D. E. and Miles, T. R. (1996) *Dyslexia at College* (3rd edition). London: Routledge.

Goodwin, V. and Thomson, B. (2004) *Making Dyslexia Work for You*. London: David Fulton Publishers.

Greetham, B. (2001) *How to Write Better Essays*. Basingtoke: Palgrave.

Jarvie, G. (2000) *Bloomsbury Grammar Guide: Grammar Made Easy*. London: Bloomsbury.

McLoughlin, D., Leather, C. and Stringer, P. (2003) *The Adult Dyslexic*. London: Whurr.

Mortimore, T. (2003) *Dyslexia and Learning Style*. London: Whurr.

Ott, P. (1997) *How to Detect and Manage Dyslexia*. London: Heinemann.

Pauk, W. (2001) *How to Study in College* (7th edition). Boston, MA: Houghton Mifflin Company.

Pleuger, G. (ed.) *The Good History Student's Handbook*. Bedford: Sempringham.

Riding, R. J. and Rayner, S. (1998) *Cognitive Styles and Learning Strategies*. London: David Fulton Publishers.

Slattery, M. and Pleuger, G. (2000) 'Essay Planning: Early Steps', in G. Pleuger (ed.) *The Good History Student's Handbook*. Bedford: Sempringham.

Truss, L. (2003) *Eats, Shoots and Leaves*. London: Profile Books.

West, T. G. (1991) *In the Mind's Eye: Visual Thinkers, Gifted People with Learning Difficulties, Computer Images and the Ironies of Creativity*. New York: Prometheus Books.

West, T. G. (2004) *Thinking Like Einstein: Returning to Our Visual Roots with the Emerging Revolution in Computer Information Visualization*. New York: Prometheus Books.

Useful websites

Concept Stew Ltd *Educational Software Design and Development* [online]. Available from www.conceptstew.co.uk/PAGES/home.html

Coping with exam stress   www.isma.org.uk/exams.htm

Study skills website of University of Southampton 2003   www.soton.ac.uk/studentsupport/ldc/academicskills/study.html

Examination arrangements   www.qub.ac.uk/disability/webpages/exam-arrangements.htm

Examination tips   www.coun.uvic.ca/learn/exam.html

Examination techniques   www.mantex.co.uk/software/skill-01.htm

Learning Technologies Ltd   www.learning-tech.co.uk

MathsisFun   www.mathsisfun.com

Purdue University's Online Writing Lab. Available at: http://owl.english.purdue.edu/

Q Notes by Jim Burke (2000) www.englishcompanion.com

Style guides

www.timesonline.co.uk/section/0,,2941,00.html

www.guardian.co.uk/styleguide/0,,,00.html?gusrc=gpd

TechDis aims to enhance provision for disabled students and staff in higher, further and specialist education and adult and community learning, through the use of technology: http://techdis.ac.uk/index.php?p=1

Index

Available Now from Lucky Duck!

Study Skills

A Teaching Programme for Students in Schools and Colleges

Pat Guy, *Individual Needs Co-ordinator*

There are many 'Do-it-Yourself' manuals for students and young people experiencing study skills problems. However, if this group of young people could study these books then they would already have the skills necessary! In order to use a self help manual the student needs internal motivation, the ability to self-instruct from text and the ability to put the learned strategy into place but these are the same attributes that these students find difficult.

In this book, Pat Guy provides a series of lesson plans making up a taught study skills course for secondary schools, sixth forms, FE colleges and Pupil Referral Units. She shows the reader how to teach, through self assessment, practice and confidence-building techniques, the techniques and self management required to achieve independent study skills.

All the activities and worksheets, including revision and exam tips for the students, are easily printable from the accompanying CD-rom.
The sessions can be delivered by teachers, tutors, Learning Mentors, or anyone whose aim is to improve attendance and achievement in older students.

Contents

A Study Skills Questionnaire / Learning Styles and Multiple Intelligences / Learning Styles and Their Relevance in Schools / Learning Style Questionnaires / Multiple Intelligences / Reading / Reading Techniques / Reading Speed / Comprehension / Reading Comprehension / Subject Specific Vocabulary / General Vocabulary / Dictionary Skills / Visualisation as an Aid to Comprehension / Memory / Memory: How to Make the Most of It / Visual and Auditory Memory Assessment / Listening and Attention / Learn Modern Foreign Language Vocabulary Kinaesthetically / Organisation / Writing/ Note Taking: Linear Note and Mind Mapping / Essays / Proof Reading / Spelling / Handwriting and Presentation / Handwriting Questionnaire / Improving Co-Ordination Skills Through Practical Activities / Presentations / Oral Presentations / Group Work / Revision and Exams / How to Revise / Exam Techniques – Pupil Sheet / Dealing With Exam Anxiety – Pupil Sheet / Appendices and Glossary

Feb 2007 • 104 pages •

Hardback (978-1-4129-2254-8) Price £60.00 • Paper (978-1-4129-2255-5) Price £18.99

www.luckyduck.co.uk
www.paulchapmanpublishing.co.uk PCP